Twayne's English Authors Series

Sylvia E. Bowman, *General Editor*

INDIANA UNIVERSITY

John Heywood

(TEAS) 92

John Heywood

By ROBERT CARL JOHNSON

Miami University (Ohio)

Twayne Publishers, Inc.   ::   New York

MANUFACTURED IN THE UNITED STATES OF AMERICA

To Marilyn

Preface

My purposes in this book are to re-evaluate the position of John Heywood in the development of English drama and to demonstrate his importance as a minor adherent to and propagandist for Christian Humanism. I discuss in the following pages all of his works, both dramatic and non-dramatic; and I hope I correct some of the sundry misunderstandings about Heywood and answer charges of dullness, obscurity, and coarseness that have been unfairly leveled at him. Too often his poetry has been dismissed before or even without being read. Burton Milligan's excellent edition of the *Works* makes the *Dialogue of Proverbs* and the epigrams readily available, and I hope it will also introduce students to this comic muse of Tudor England. The dramatic works, however, are only available in Farmer's edition; a definitive modern edition is an obvious necessity. Except for Milligan's edition of the *Works,* Heywood's poetry is not readily accessible; therefore, I have quoted extensively from the plays and poem when analyzing them. Most readers will probably agree that the long, unsuccessful *Spider and the Fly* is best left unread even if they obtain it; the allegory, obscure in Heywood's day, is even more bewildering now.

I have placed severe limits on the first chapter. It is too easy to become involved with the events of that colorful period —early Tudor England—or to see the sorting out of the various grants and payments to Heywood as an end in itself. This book pretends to be neither a history nor a biography, but Chapter 1 sketches the historical background, outlining the problems of Henry VIII and his court. Since Heywood was intimately connected with the court throughout his adult life, we must have some knowledge of the history of the period. At the same time, I survey the somewhat confusing records of Heywood's life in an attempt to delineate his function at court. The chronological table, moreover, offers a convenient summary of the important dates in Heywood's life.

The largest part of the book, which I have divided into three chapters, critically analyzes Heywood's poetry and plays. Chapter 2 discusses the non-dramatic works, and Chapter 3 reviews the six plays usually assigned to Heywood. I suggest a possible order of composition and reasons for believing that Heywood definitely wrote all six plays.

Although Heywood's importance in Tudor drama is connected with his discovery of French farce, I do not discuss sources in Chapter 3; but I do devote Chapter 4 to an analysis of his use of sources. In the last chapter I give reasons both for and against the assigning of *Gentleness and Nobility* to Heywood and discuss some of the contemporary plays, a discussion which should emphasize Heywood's unique qualities. It is, of course, impossible to survey all of Tudor drama; but a brief sketch of the surrounding drama is necessary in order to make some final statements about Heywood's influence upon later literature and about his stature within his particular period. Moreover, I have used the notes for developing some of my arguments and occasionally for a summary of prior scholarship in order to produce a more readable text.

Finally I must express my thanks to several who have helped with this book. My debt to past scholars should be sufficiently evident in my notes and bibliography, but there are other less obvious debts. To my indefatigable wife who typed the manuscript and helped proofread special thanks are due. Professors Burton Milligan and Allan Holaday, both of the University of Illinois, are in many ways the inspiration for this book. Tudor England is alive and exciting to me because of people who lived then, John Heywood and Thomas More, to name only two, and because of these teachers who first introduced me to the period. Both have that warm sense of humor that was Heywood's most endearing characteristic.

—ROBERT CARL JOHNSON

Miami University (Ohio)

Contents

Contents

Chronology

1485 Accession of Henry VII.

1497 Birth of John Heywood.

1509 Death of Henry VII; accession of Henry VIII.

1519 Heywood receives quarterly wages 100s. No duties mentioned.

1520 Receives quarterly wages 100s. as court singer.

1521 Heywood receives a royal grant of 10 marks from the manors of Makesey and Torpel in Northamptonshire; another grant of 7 marks from the manor of Haydon, Essex.

1523 Heywood admitted to the liberties of the city of London.

1526 Receives payment of £6, 13s. 4d.; listed as player of the virginals.

1528 Receives pension of £10 per year as player of the virginals; payment seems to have continued until 1550. He was also appointed steward of the king's chamber.

1529 Fall of Cardinal Wolsey; Thomas More becomes Chancellor.

1530 Ellis Heywood born; Heywood had married Eliza Rastell sometime between 1523 and 1529.

1531 Henry the Supreme Head of the English Church.

1533 Thomas Cranmer becomes Archbishop of Canterbury; Act in Restraint of Appeals; Henry marries Anne Boleyn. Heywood receives a New Year's gift of plate from Henry VIII. John Rastell prints *Gentleness and Nobility;* William Rastell prints *The Pardoner and the Friar; Love; Weather;* and either now or on February 12, 1534, *Johan Johan.*

1534 Heywood writes poem praising Princess Mary. Acts of Succession and Supremacy.

1535 Execution of More and John Fisher; Jasper Heywood born.

1536 Suppression of the monasteries; Pilgrimage of Grace.

1538 Heywood presents an interlude with "his children" before Princess Mary.

1539 Statute of VI Articles. Heywood produces mask of Arthur's Knights at court.

1540 Heywood receives twenty-one-year lease on Broke Hall, Essex, at £10.

1544 Heywood, involved in the plot to overthrow Archbishop Cranmer, is accused of treason and imprisoned; by publicly recanting, he was pardoned and his lands and annuities were restored. *The Four PP* was published sometime between 1543 and 1547 by William Middleton.

1546   T. Berthelet prints *Dialogue of Proverbs*.

1547   Death of Henry VIII; accession of Edward VI; Duke of Somerset becomes Protector.

1549   Kett's rebellion.

1550   *An hundred Epigrammes*.

1552   Heywood receives payment of 30s. for his part in an entertainment before Princess Elizabeth. Reappointed as steward of the king's chamber; salary increased to £40.

1553   Heywood's play and others to be performed before Edward; postponed because of the King's illness. Edward VI dies; accession of Mary. Heywood receives £50 in addition to his regular salary. Delivers an oration in Latin and English during Mary's coronation procession.

1554   Marriage of Mary and Philip. Heywood celebrates the marriage with a poem; receives lands in Kent from Mary.

1555   Reappointed as steward of queen's chamber; salary increased to £50. *Epigrams upon Proverbs*.

1556   T. Powell prints *The Spider and the Fly*.

1558   Heywood resigns as steward of the queen's chamber, but receives lands in Yorkshire and a lease for Bolmer manor for 40 years. Death of Mary; accession of Elizabeth I.

1559   Heywood participates in an entertainment for Elizabeth at Nonesuch. Acts of Uniformity and Supremacy.

1560   *A fourth hundred of Epygrams* printed by T. Berthelet.

1562   Thomas Powell publishes Heywood's *Works*.

1563   XXXIX Articles.

1564   Heywood leaves England for exile; mentioned in Rastell's will.

1571   Nicholus Sanderus mentions Heywood as one of the English Catholics living in exile. His lands in Kent confiscated.

1574   Thomas Wilson sees Heywood at Malines about returning to England.

1575   Heywood writes to Lord Burleigh requesting the continuation of his income.

1576   Heywood living at Jesuit College at Antwerp.

1578   Heywood caught up in the religious turmoil at Antwerp. He escapes to Louvain, but dies later this year.

CHAPTER 1

The Historical Background

I *The Two Henries*

J OHN HEYWOOD is one of those fascinating minor figures
that cavort in the shadows cast by the Chaucers, the Shake-
speares, and the Johnsons. In Heywood's case, Erasmus, Sir
Thomas More, Henry VIII, Cardinal Wolsey, and Queen Mary
are the dominant figures of the age; but Heywood played his
lesser role with consummate skill, contributing in his small way
the humor that such an age sorely needed.

Heywood's life spans the turmoil of English history in the
early sixteenth century. At his birth in 1497 Henry VII was on
the throne, having already ruled for twelve years. The Battle of
Bosworth Field had finally resolved the feuding parties in that
lengthy War of the Roses. Henry's marriage to Elizabeth of York
united the two factions in marriage and allayed all fears of any
massacre of the Yorkist followers. His policies of leniency
strengthened the people's confidence in the central monarchy;
indeed, Henry's primary contribution to English history is that
he developed in his twenty-four-year reign a strong central
monarchy capable of suppressing rebellions of rival claimants
without oppressive taxation or a large standing army.

As a result, he developed within his subjects a sense of reliance
upon the central authority; and, for the first time, the noble class
no longer controlled the king. The rise of the middle class,
coupled with the hostility of both the lower class and that of
Henry himself, resulted in a new social and political climate in
England. Henry gave more authority to the local justices of
peace and strengthened the entire administrative system. All
of Henry's reforms were, of course, made more palatable by the
memories of the chaos of the preceding years.

It is easier to state Henry VII's achievements in a negative way, for he was not the dominant and controversial ruler that Henry VIII was. Henry VII's most important achievement was his very survival, one which established the Tudor dynasty. He also rescued the crown from bankruptcy, an achievement which has been overglamorized by the tradition that he was an economical ruler who bequeathed to his son a fortune which he squandered. Henry VII's secret was skillful organization—he established a ruling class or civil service—which resulted in economy. A glance at his court expenditures reveals that he lived in a grand manner.

If we allow for the hyperbole that infects any funeral elegy, we can get a glimpse of Henry's character from Bishop Fisher's sermon:

. . . his polytyque wysedome in gouernaunce it was synguler, his wytte alway quycke and redy, his reason pyththy and substancyall, his memory fresshe and holdynge, his experyence notable, his counseylles fortunate and taken by wyse delyberacyon, his speche gracyous in dyuerse languages, his persone goodly and amyable, his naturall compleccyon of the purest myxture, his yssue fayre and in good nombre, leages and confyderyes he hadde with all crysten prynces, his mighty power was dredde euery where, not onely within his realme but without also, his people were to hym in as humble subgeccyon as ever they were to kynge, his londe many a day in peas and tranquyllyte, his prosperyte in batayle ayenst his enemyes was meruaylous, his delynge in tyme of perylles and daungers was colde and sobre with grete hardynesse. If ony treason were conspyred ayenst hym it came out wonderfully, his treasour and rychesse incomparable, his buyldynges mooste goodly and after the newest cast all of pleasure.[1]

Here we have it all: the centralization of government, the respect for the monarch, the peace after years of war, the comparative prosperity after chaotic years of internal upheaval. Henry thus developed the same power as the kings on the Continent, but he did it with the help of the people, not in spite of them. He is representative of what has been termed the "new monarchy."

Of primary concern was the succession upon Henry's death. Arthur, the Prince of Wales, died young; so the crown passed to his second son who became Henry VIII. This continuation of the dynasty was important since Henry's claim to the throne in 1485 had been negligible. If he had not been able to pass his crown to a legitimate son, the country might have again been plunged into civil war. Instead, Henry VIII ruled from 1509 to 1547, firmly entrenching both his personal rule and the Tudor dynasty.

Today it is easy to overlook the importance of the monarch in the historical and literary developments of a period. Both Henry (1509-47) and Elizabeth (1558-1603) dominated their particular age. Each gave the age its distinctive character that affects, in many cases very noticeably, the literature (in that very general sense that includes sermons, broadside ballads, and polemic pamphlets). It is a century of personal rule, and we appreciate the age through an understanding of the dominant personalities.

The reign of Henry VIII divides into two parts. In the first part he abdicated his rule to his close counselor, Cardinal Wolsey. With the fall of Wolsey, Henry firmly grasped the reins of government and was in firm control of England until his death, even attempting to maintain control after death by setting up the order of succession. Christopher Morris has called Henry a "Renaissance 'magnifico,'"[2] and such a cryptic phrase summarizes the impression Henry made on his contemporaries. Every inch the king, he coupled a handsome figure with both athletic grace and intellectual prowess, especially in languages and theology. Such qualities overshadowed an extreme egotism and capriciousness, characteristics that dominated the latter period of his rule. A report written in 1519 by the Venetian ambassador, Giustinian, to the English court sketches the salient features of Henry: "He is very accomplished; a good musician; composes well; is a most capital horseman; a fine jouster; speaks good French, Latin, and Spanish; is very religious; hears three masses daily when he hunts, and sometimes five on other days: he hears the *office* every day in the Queen's chamber, that is to say vespers and compline."[3]

Heywood's life revolved around the monarchy; he complemented Henry's interest in music and produced plays and entertainments for the young king. And he remained a constant attendant at the court of three rulers until he left England for exile in France sometime after the accession of Elizabeth.

Although we have no concrete knowledge of Heywood's birth or parentage, he was probably one of the new middle class that had raised itself into new prominence. Heywood was born in London in 1497, for he writes from exile to Lord Burghley in 1575 and refers to himself as being then seventy-eight years old.

Although some controversy surrounds his place of birth, the
evidence points to London; for both of Heywood's early
biographers—Bishop Bale and John Pitseus—list London as his
birthplace. The confusion stems from the misinterpretation of a
passage in Henry Peacham's *The Compleat Gentleman,* where
Peacham writes that Heywood wrote his epigrams at North
Mims. He does not imply that Heywood was necessarily born
there: ". . . and merry Iohn Heywood, who wrote his Epigrammes, as also Sir Thomas More his Vtopia, in the parish
wherein I was borne; where either of them dwelt, and had
faire possessions."[4] It is difficult to determine when Heywood
first entered court circles. Contemporary records are sparse, and
speculation has no firm basis. John Payne Collier, A. W. Ward
(*Dictionary of National Biography*), and C. W. Wallace (*Evolution of the English Drama*) suggest that Heywood was a
member of the Chapel Royal as a choirboy, but his name does
not appear on any contemporary records. Anthony à Wood, who
claims that Heywood was briefly a student at Broadgates, Oxford, explains the brevity of his scholastic career thus: "But the
crabbedness of logic not suiting with his airy genie, he retired
to his native place, and became noted to all witty men, especially
to sir Tho. More. . . ."[5]

Since Broadgates did not keep records until 1570, Anthony à
Wood's statement can not be disproved. *Witty and Witless,* one
of Heywood's earliest dramatic works, may reflect a schoolboy's
concerns for abstractions and debates, but there is little in any
of his other dramatic works that suggests a scholarly life. Moreover, neither John Pitseus, Bishop Bale, nor any other contemporaries of Heywood mentions a scholastic career or refers to
Heywood as student or scholar. The legal quibbling in *The
Spider and the Fly* does not reflect the brief stay at Broadgates.
Two of his epigrams, however, manifest a familiarity with some
aspects of university life:

> Alas poore verdingates must lie in the streete:
> To house them, no doore in the citee made meete.
> Syns at our narow doores they in can not win,
> Send them to Oxforde, at Brodegates to get in.[6]

> Testons be gone to Oxforde, god be their speede:
> To studie in Brasenose there to proceede (V, 63).

It would be more profitable to understand the meaning of the
second part of Anthony à Wood's statement. That Heywood was

a close friend of Sir Thomas More is a well-known fact. Some time during the 1520's Heywood married Eliza Rastell, whose father, John Rastell, had married Sir Thomas More's sister; so Heywood was an intimate member of the More-Rastell circle. How early he became an intimate of More is difficult to say, but Heywood's name is mentioned prominently at the end of William Roper's biography of More: "Which matter was by the same Sir Thomas Elyot to myself, to my wife, to Master Clement and his wife to Master John Heywood and his wife, and unto divers other his friends accordinly reported."[7] And John Pitseus refers to Heywood and More thus: "Thomae Moro multis annis familiarissimus" (for many years an intimate friend of Thomas More).

That Heywood was not an original thinker is obvious to any reader of his works, but that he was a product of his time and a reflection of his environment I hope to make clear in subsequent chapters. And his environment was substantially molded by Sir Thomas More; indeed, Heywood may have been one of the young men that More surrounded himself with before he entered the service of the king. Professor Routh writes of this coterie: "The group of young people gathered together in the famous house at Chelsea were devoted to More and deeply influenced by his teaching. Their literary and dramatic talents presented an interesting aspect of Renaissance culture in England. Among the more intimate members of the group were the Rastells, Heywoods, and Clements, some of whom were dispersed into exile after the death of More, when the religious strife darkened the English scene."[8]

More entered the service of Henry VIII in 1519, and the first definite reference to John Heywood in the court records occurs in the same year where he is the recipient of 100s. No duties are mentioned, but in 1520 he again received 100s: "Item for John Hajwoode synger wages. . . . Cs."[9] We can assume, since the payment is similar, that he came to the court as a singer or entertainer. John Payne Collier first pointed out an earlier payment to a John Heywood on January 6, 1515;[10] however, no duties are listed, and the payment is 8d a day. Collier and others have lifted the entry out of context, and it is more likely that this is another Heywood, a yeoman who performed a particular service. There are several other recipients in the same entry who are referred to as yeomen. At any rate, there is no

mention of any Heywood from 1515 to 1519. Although some
biographers assume that he remained at court during this time,
I insist that he did not come to court until 1519 and that,
before 1519, he was a protégé of Thomas More.

Because of his relationship with More, Heywood must have
come under the influence of the new humanistic spirit that
dominated the early sixteenth century. Erasmus himself, as early
as 1499, had written of the English humanists:

I have met with so much kindness and so much learning—not super-
ficial either, but intelligent and accurate—both Latin and Greek, that
but for the curiosity of seeing it, I do not now so much care for Italy.
When I hear my Colet, I seem to be listening to Plato himself. In
Grocyn, who does not marvel at such perfection of learning? What
can be more acute, profound and delicate than the judgement of
Linacre? What has nature ever created more sweet, more endearing,
more happy than the genius of Thomas More? It is marvellous how
general and abundant is the harvest of ancient learning in this
country.[11]

Influenced by traveling to the Renaissance countries of Italy
and France and by the presence of foreign scholars at the court
and at Oxford—the most important influence being Erasmus
himself—the English intellectual gradually developed a new
critical, analytical spirit, a new awareness of the past that
included the revival of Classical studies. An atmosphere of
exploration, of the penetrating question, and of criticism per-
meates the writings and activities of these men. It is not simply
a revival of learning, a rediscovery of the Classics, but also a
new methodology. Erasmus translated the New Testament,
satirized the Church in *The Praise of Folly,* and outlined the
proper training for a Christian ruler *(The Education of a
Christian Prince).* John Colet, a clergyman, founded the famous
St. Paul's School, of which William Lyly, the author of a new
Latin grammar, was the first headmaster. William Grocyn was a
theological scholar, and Thomas Linacre applied the new learning
to medicine. Thomas More, the best known of the early English
humanists, called for a new form of government in *Utopia.* Each
of these efforts reflects the new struggle, the new interest in man.

Pearl Hogrefe has discussed at length how the members of
More's circle shared common ideas about nobility, law, government, education, and religious reform;[12] and later in this book
we shall see how Heywood's plays reflect to some extent these
basic ideas.

When Heywood and More entered the court in 1519 Henry was not the actual ruler of England, for that same year the Venetian ambassador, Giustinian, wrote of Cardinal Wolsey: "This Cardinal is the person who rules both the King and the entire Kingdom."[13] He then relates the famous anecdote of the change in the Cardinal's phrasing of the various commands from "His Majesty will do so and so" to "We will do so and so" and finally to "I will do so and so."

If Henry VIII represents the ideal of Tudor kingliness, Wolsey represents the paradoxical qualities of the Catholic Church. Wolsey was at the same time the secular and the clerical power of England. George Cavendish, who has captured the complex personality of the Cardinal in his biography, interprets Wolsey's life as a panoramic morality play with Pride as the villain. Writing soon after Wolsey's death, Cavendish depicts with some literary skill the ostentatious, extravagant career of his lord by recording the sumptuous banquets and his splendid dress. What is missing from the biography, and also from the man himself, is a spiritual side. The reader leaves the biography with the impression of a man consumed by ambition and the lust for power. An astute politician, he manipulated not only the affairs of state, but also schemed to achieve his personal goal—the Papacy. Twice while Wolsey was at his height—in 1521 and 1523—the Papacy was vacant, and Wolsey hoped for brief moments that he might become Pope, personally urging his election upon the Cardinals at Rome.

As a statesman, he occasionally employed the doctrine of a balance of power. By siding with the weaker states, England assured itself at least an uneasy peace although it was involved in a series of minor skirmishes. To preserve a balance of power, England had joined Spain in a war against France in 1513; but Henry VIII made peace with France in 1514. After the French victory in Italy in 1518, Wolsey was instrumental in framing a treaty of universal peace, a tribute more to his prestige than a reflection of the realities of the political turmoil on the Continent; for the treaty dissolved a few months after its signing when Maximilian's death left vacant the throne of the Holy Roman Empire, to which both Francis of France and Charles of Spain aspired.

When Charles became emperor, England found itself courted by both rulers; Wolsey relished his position of power seeing the opportunities for both national and personal aggrandizement. In 1520 Charles visited England to see Wolsey and Henry, and later that same year Henry sailed to France to meet Francis at the "Field of Cloth of Gold"; the splendor of this meeting is reflected in its traditional name. Forced finally to choose, Wolsey sided with Charles; for, since he wished to become Pope, the influence of Spain, he reasoned, would be greater when the Papacy became vacant.

Yet by 1525—after Wolsey had failed to become Pope— England was at odds with its former ally, and these strained relations with the native country of Henry's wife, Catherine, helped lead to the English Reformation. In 1525 Charles' forces in the Battle of Pavia had utterly routed the French army, and France was now at the mercy of the Emperor. When Wolsey and England moved to restore a balance of power, the situation was complicated by the sack of Rome in 1527 and by Henry's growing impatience for a divorce. Although this brief survey can not do justice to the complexities of the situation, the position and prestige of Wolsey should be evident. Cavendish sums up Wolsey's power in the following statement:

Thus in great honor, triumph, and glory he reigned a long season, ruling all thing within this realm appertaining unto the King by his wisdom, and also all other weighty matters of foreign regions with whom the King and this realm had any occasion to intermeddle. All ambassadors of foreign potentates were alway dispatched by his discretion, to whom they had always access for their dispatch. His house was also always resorted [to] and furnished with noblemen, gentlemen, and other persons with going and coming in and out, feasting and banqueting all ambassadors divers times and other strangers right nobly.[14]

It should be clear that the court in which Heywood entertained was also Wolsey's. One of Heywood's plays, *The Weather*, alludes to the problem of the ruler of a state and to the problems of keeping the various social and occupational factions satisfied. The play can be read as a compliment to Henry VIII, but it should be clear that Wolsey was the real ruler. In his position as clerical leader Wolsey might also have been affected by Heywood's farces which attack the general corruptions of the church. But, before the divorce question became critical, Henry's court must have enjoyed such exposures of the corrupt Pardoners and Friars, just as Chaucer's contemporaries did.

A firm Catholic partisan, Heywood mirrors both the self-reforming, self-critical spirit of some Renaissance churchmen and the loyalty and devotion of the church's adherents. He describes his personality and suggests his occupation in one of his poems:

> Art thou Heywood with the mad mery wit?
> Ye forsooth maister, that same is euen hit.
> Art thou Heywood that applieth mirth more then thrift?
> Ye sir, I take mery mirth a golden gift.
> Art thou Heywood that hath made many mad plaies?
> Ye many plaies, fewe good workes in all my daies.
> Art thou Heywood that hath made men mery long?
> Ye: and will, if I be made mery among.
> Art thou Heywood that woulde be made mery now?
> Ye sir: helpe me to it now I beseche you. (V, 100)

What Heywood's court function was it is difficult to determine, but he was no court jester nor was he a respected counselor: "It is most probable he had no special position at court but was only a licensed favourite, or a personal attendant, with a nominal role like that of *dapifer camerae* (steward of the royal chamber) or *sewer*, one who was expected to be a literary and musical handyman and on occasion to be the actor-manager at the Court."[15] Heywood distinguished himself as a musician, singer, dramatist, and "mad merry wit"; for his success in his position as entertainer can be judged by his early reputation. Bishop Bale, writing in 1557, praised Heywood's musical and poetic powers and listed such activities as producing dances, plays, comic masks, and other frivolous shows. "Joannes Heyvuode . . . musices ac rhythmicae artis in sua lingua studiosus, & siue doctrina ingeniosus, pro choreis post comessationes & epulas hilariter ducendis, spectaculis, ludis, aut personatis ludicris exhibendis, alijsque uanitatibus fouendis, multum laborabat. . . .[16]

And John Pitseus elaborated upon Heywood's achievements in 1619: "Vir pius, vtcumque doctus, valde ingeniosus, Musices tam vocalis, quam instrumentalis peritus, elegans in Poesi, & plus quam credi potest, in familiari colloquio lepidus atque facetus (A godly man, howsoever learned, very ingenious, so gifted with song, so skilled with instruments, elegant in poetry and more so to be believed in pleasant and witty colloquial pieces)."[17] Moreover, that Heywood was a successful entertainer is evident from the grants of both land and money he received during his years at court. To delineate his position any more specifically than these men have done is merely to enter into random speculation.

We can assume, although the records of this period are incomplete, that—after his introduction to court as a young man of twenty-two—he received a specific, regular wage. His dramatic activities—the writing that gained him literary importance—were but one part of his activities. Instead, it seems more likely that the sundry jobs that Bishop Bale listed in his biography occupied most of Heywood's time. The various payments over a span of forty years suggest his varied talents.

In 1520 the records list him as a singer; in 1526 as "player of the virginals"; and in 1528 he received a life appointment as *dapifer camerae* or steward of the royal chamber, a position which was renewed with increasing salary under both Edward and Mary.[18] As early as 1521 he received his first manorial grant—ten marks from the manor of Makesey and Torpel in Northhampton.[19]

Sometime in the 1520's Heywood married Eliza Rastell. Ellis Heywood was born in 1530, so that we can place the marriage as late as 1529, although A. W. Reed has suggested it took place as early as 1523.[20] Eliza's brother, William Rastell, was the printer who published four of Heywood's plays—*Pardoner and Friar, Play of Love, Play of Weather,* and *Johan Johan* in 1533. Heywood's main dramatic activity then is concentrated in this initial period of court activity before Henry VIII's formal break with Rome. Both Heywood and William Rastell remained loyal to Catholicism and to Sir Thomas More; but John Rastell, the father and also a dramatist, was converted to the Protestant side by John Firth, against whom both he and More had addressed polemical pamphlets.

II *The Divorce Problem*

Finally, the crisis that Wolsey could not handle arose; for Henry was concerned about the succession to his throne. His wife, Catherine, had born him only one child, Mary. A series of miscarriages and stillbirths now plagued Henry's conscience, and he questioned, I think we can say sincerely, the validity of his marriage since Catherine had been married to Arthur, Henry's brother. (The church considered a sister-in-law as close a relation as an actual sister.) To marry his sister-in-law in

1509, Henry had had to receive a special dispensation from the Pope. Coupled with these fears of the consequences of a queen on the English throne and his doubts of the legality of his marriage was his love for a lady of the court, Anne Boleyn. The result was that Wolsey was commissioned to secure a divorce for Henry.

It is easy to oversimplify the break with Rome. Henry could have married Anne Boleyn without the political maneuvering that took place. The Pope several times hinted that Wolsey might handle the matter under his own jurisdiction; but Wolsey, sensing an opportunity for more power, pressed Clement VII to grant the papal dispensation. But Clement was reluctant to reverse the act of a former Pope, and he was also disinclined to anger Catherine's Spanish friends and relatives. Thus, the divorce proceedings dragged through interminable inquiries and delays, finally exhausting Henry's patience.

As a result, Henry replaced Wolsey as Chancellor with Sir Thomas More in 1529 and called Parliament into session that same year to aid him in seeking a divorce in the English courts. In four years (1530-34) Henry established the English Reformation. That it was achieved so rapidly and so peacefully indicates the corrupt and abusive practices of the church prior to 1530, a subject to which Heywood often directs his scathing pen. The sacred awe for Rome that earlier might have controlled a less spirited rebellion no longer existed. Nor could Charles of Spain come to the rescue of his aunt, Catherine, for he was occupied with distant battles in Italy and France. Coupled with these factors was a growing spirit of nationalism that rebelled at any outside interference. The time was apt, therefore, for Henry's move; Parliament and the people were docile.

As a first step, Henry took from the Pope the first year's revenues of each bishopric. More important, he passed the Act of Appeals in 1533 which required all ecclesiastical cases to be tried in an English court—a law that enabled the divorce proceedings to be tried by Archbishop Cranmer. Thus Henry annulled his own marriage; Catherine was no longer queen; Anne Boleyn replaced her on the throne and within the year gave birth to Princess Elizabeth.

In 1534 the Act of Supremacy declared Henry Supreme Head of the Church—an act that was the most violent break from the old order. Recognizing the implications of such an act, Thomas

More and John Fisher refused to take the oath and were promptly executed. Anne Boleyn soon followed them to the block, and the capricious Henry married Jane Seymour. Meanwhile, he more firmly entrenched the new order by dissolving the monasteries. The gain from such an act was twofold: first, the revenue which the government treasury so badly needed; second, the good will he gained from those noblemen who benefited from the dissolution. For the most part there was little opposition, especially in the South; but in the North a lawyer, Robert Aske, organized an armed protest which has been labeled the "Pilgrimage of Grace." Initially successful, the revolt was abortive; and Robert Aske was executed for his role.

The separation of England from Rome was Henry's burst of glory. After he dissolved the monasteries, his energy was spent; and to trace his frantic search for an heir and his three subsequent marriages is to delve into personalities. His important contribution is political and religious. The Henrican church is Protestant only in the sense that it broke from Rome, for the Six Articles of Faith passed in 1539 illustrate the early religious tone of the Anglican Church. These acts provided stringent penalties for those who denied transubstantiation, the power of confession, the value of clerical celibacy, and the restriction of wine to the clergy in the communion. But against these Catholic doctrines were Henry's insistence upon private interpretation of the Bible and his restrictions upon papal jurisdiction.

For a loyal Catholic and personal attendant upon the king, such as Heywood, the early 1530's were a period of turmoil. Since More and Bishop Fisher were executed for their beliefs, we are tempted to ask how Heywood was not only able to stay alive but also to maintain his position at court. The records offer little basis for speculation. There is a New Year's gift in 1533 of plate to a Heywood, who I assume is our subject—the year that Archbishop Cranmer announced Henry's divorce. We need hardly stress that 1533 witnessed the publication of four of Heywood's plays, two of which, *The Pardoner and the Friar* and *Johan Johan*, satirize the abuses of the Catholic Church. I insist, however, that the plays were written earlier; for Heywood surely would not have contributed ammunition for the battle at this crucial moment, although the publication of his works at this time obviously would have done nothing to harm his relationship with Henry VIII. I will discuss the dating of the plays in Chapter 3.

Heywood's next recorded activity is in 1538 when he presented a play with a group of children before Princess Mary: "Item geuen to Haywood playeing an enterlude with his Children bifore my ladys grace . . . xls."[21] The entry, because it gives us no idea about the play itself, poses the problem concerning Heywood's relationship with a children's acting group. Does the phrase "with his Children" indicate that Heywood is in charge of the company or merely that this children's group performed one of Heywood's plays written especially for the occasion? The entry can not even be used to prove authorship of this unknown play. Several times—in 1538, 1552, 1553, and 1559—Heywood is connected with an unspecified children's group, which has been variously identified as the children of the Chapel Royal and the boys of St. Paul's who "probably performed his plays."[22] Bolwell's more conservative analysis deserves to be quoted:

The data at hand, then, do not favor the belief that Heywood was officially connected with either the Chapel or the St. Paul's schools. It is much safer to assume, and there is nothing to contradict the assumption, that Heywood was never connected with either institution as a master of boys, but that he frequently acted as a master of festivities, perhaps also as a dramatic "coach" for these and other companies of boys. None of the men whom we know to have been masters of children was so loaded with court duties; and this is a strong argument against Heywood's having constant charge of a band of children which in all probability would have taken most of his time.[23]

Perhaps in this period Heywood centered his attention upon the disgraced Mary, for a poem praising her has been preserved in part in *Tottell's Miscellany*. The last stanza suggests that it was written in 1534 when Mary was eighteen:

> And Mary was her name, weete ye,
> With these graces indued,
> At eighteene yeares, so flourysht shee,
> So doth his meane conclude.

The praise is standard, the poetry inferior; but a second version does show slight improvement. The first stanza is an excellent example:

> Geve place, ye ladyes, all bee gone,
> Showe not your selves at all.

For whye? behoulde, there cumeth one
Whose face yours all blanke shall.

Give place, yea ladies, and be gone,
Boast not your selves at all,
For heere at hand approachethe one
Whose face will staine you all.
                              (Milligan, 250-54)

To write such a poem in 1534 manifests a certain loyalty, one
which was rewarded when Mary finally came to the throne; but
in 1534 it was dangerous to support the young Princess who had
not yet been reconciled with her father and indeed had actually
been banished to the country, not being permitted to join the
court. Bolwell has even suggested that Heywood may have been
a member of Mary's retinue during this period.[24] Heywood may
also have been working on *The Spider and the Fly* in the late
1530's, a work which he did not publish until Mary was queen.
If the Pilgrimage of Grace (September, 1536) is the inspiration
for his long allegorical poem, Heywood was probably working
on the poem after that date.

In 1539 Heywood presented a mask of Arthur's Knights at
court.[25] The work, of course, is not extant; but the court record
gives us another glimpse of Heywood performing those duties
that Bishop Bale describes. Indeed, the directing and producing
of such masks and court entertainments seem to be Heywood's
most important contribution to Henry's court. Those dramatic
efforts—the simple interludes and farces—which ensured him
a place in the development of dramatic literature give us a
distorted impression of his true function as a court entertainer.

But Heywood was also engaged in non-dramatic activities.
His loyalty to the Catholic faith caused him to work against
the spread of Protestantism and to become involved in the
plot against Archbishop Cranmer. As I mentioned above, the
Six Articles instituted in 1539 were strongly Catholic in nature;
and Protestant Cranmer was not reporting the frequent violations
of these articles. Thus a group, headed by the pro-Catholic
Germain Gardiner and including John Heywood, accused Cranmer of heresy. Henry, not deceived by this group's bias,
appointed Cranmer himself to head an investigation into the
charges. The result was imprisonment for Heywood in 1543
for his part in a plot to overthrow Cranmer and to deny the
supremacy of the King. Gardiner was eventually executed, but

the recantation of Heywood which saved him from a like fate is described by John Foxe: "The same year followed the recantation of John Heywood; who although he was attached for treason, for denying the king's supremacy, yet, using the clemency of the king, upon his better reformation and amendment, he made an open and solemn recantation in the face of all the people, abandoning and renouncing the pope's usurped supremacy, and confessing the king to be chief supreme head and governor of this church of England, all foreign authority and jurisdiction being excluded."[26]

But perhaps more important for our attempt to understand Heywood as his contemporaries did is Sir John Harington's account of the recantation: "What think you by Haywood, that escaped hanging with his mirth? The king being graciously and (as I think) truly persuaded that a man that wrote so pleasant and harmless verses, could not have any harmful conceit against his proceedings; and so by the honest motion of a gentleman of his chamber, saved him from the jerk of the six stringed whip."[27] Without the public recantation, it is unlikely, however, that Heywood's wit would have saved him. But Heywood does not seem to have suffered from his flirtation with treason, for all of his lands and grants were restored to him.

III *Edward and Mary*

When Henry died in 1547, his son Edward was heir to the throne according to Henry's expressed desires. Since Edward was too young to rule in his own right, his uncle, the Duke of Somerset, became regent. A strong Protestant, the Duke ensured the widening of the Rome-England separation. Repealing the Six Articles of 1539, Parliament endorsed forty-two more Protestant articles. During Edward's reign the first Book of Common Prayer was issued, an additional entrenchment of the Protestant tradition.

The period was also one of economic unrest. The wool trade was prospering; and, to ensure grazing land, the wealthier landowners were enclosing their lands, thus depriving the lower classes of the traditional commons lands. This confiscation of land, along with the debasing of coins—a practice started in Henry VIII's time—produced an economic crisis and finally a peasants' revolt, Kett's rebellion in 1549. Again the revolt failed, but it was the cause of Somerset's fall from power. The Earl of Warwick used his crushing of this rebellion as a means of wresting power from Somerset, who was already unpopular because of the economic crisis.

Heywood here found more material for his allegorical poem, *The Spider and the Fly*. In this poem Heywood concerns himself at length with the social conditions of England, specifically with the raising of rents and the enclosing of lands. Although it is difficult to identify accurately the various historical events and personages hidden beneath the allegory, Heywood's genuine concern with such social problems is obvious.

The accession of Edward did little to change Heywood's position at court. We find him preparing entertainments, and he is reappointed steward at an increase in salary. Heywood prepared a play for the young king around Easter, 1553; but it was postponed because of Edward's illness. The court entertainers appear to have been particularly active immediately before the king's death. Heywood's play—"A play of the state of Ierland and another of childerne sett owte by Mr. haywood" —is but one of several masks and entertainments found in the one entry.[28] Heywood's play demanded two more parts than *Weather*; at least one note refers to twelve boys, although unfortunately it suggests nothing about the play itself: "John Robertes for xxiiij[ti] ells of lockeram for the making of xij cotes for the boyes in heywoodes playe at xij[d] y[e] ell."[29] The student of Heywood must lament the fact that no trace of these entertainments survives.

The drift toward Protestantism was abruptly halted when Edward died in 1553 a few months before his sixteenth birthday. Mary, a religious zealot, came to the throne with a burning desire to reunite England with Rome. The epithet "Bloody Mary" is, however, somewhat misleading as she did not persecute the Protestants more than they had formerly persecuted Catholics. She suffers from the picture painted of her by later Protestant writers, especially Foxe in his *Book of Martyrs* and through association with Bishop Bonner, a symbol of oppression to almost all early Elizabethans. Her tragedy is that she completely misinterpreted—or perhaps ignored—the attitude of the English people. In the first place, they did not share her zealous devotion to Rome; they were quite willing to retreat from the extreme Protestantism of Edward but were hardly prepared to enter again into a union with Rome. Yet as Mary pressed ahead, Parliament repealed all of the statutes passed during Edward's reign; Mary received the papal embassy and restored the

Catholic form of worship. She even comtemplated restoring the monasteries, but opposition was too strong.

Second, to ensure a continuation of Catholic rule, she arranged a marriage with Phillip II of Spain, a union that was unpopular enough to cause several rebellions. Thomas Wyatt was the leader of the most serious rebellion, but it too was crushed. Phillip virtually ignored his wife, while Mary wishfully imagined herself carrying the next king of England in her womb. Never a well woman, she died still believing she was pregnant. Since Parliament had forbidden Phillip to ever occupy the English throne, the crown passed to Elizabeth; and the country again hung in the balance between Catholicism and Protestantism.

It was Mary's accession that raised Heywood to the height of his power. Long loyal to the Queen—the poem in praise of her written in 1534 may be used to indicate the earliest date of their intimacy—Heywood was well rewarded when Mary finally ascended the throne. Heywood greeted her ascension with "an Oration in Latine and English"[30] while sitting under a vine in Paul's Churchyard. He rejoiced in the marriage of those two Catholic monarchs, Mary and Phillip, in 1554 by penning upon the occasion a poem—one of poor poetic quality and of fatuous flattery.

The poem suggests Heywood's rapturous state in Mary's England and is the attempt of a devoted follower to justify her unpopular marriage. Phillip is the beautiful eagle; Mary, the lion. The allegory opens with the eagle leaving his own land, not alighting until he has found the beautiful rose, "both red and whight." He chooses as his mate the lion; Heywood hastens to justify such an incongruous choice. The following stanzas suggest the tasteless, strained quality of the entire poem:

> A birde, a beast to make to choose,
> Namelie, the beaste most furious,
> It may seeme straunge, and so it doose,
> And to this birde iniurious.
> It seemthe a case right curious
> To make construction in suche sens
> As may stande for this birds defens.

> But marke, this lion, so by name,
> Is properlie a lambe tassyne,
> No lion wilde, a lion tame,
> No rampant lion masculyne,
> The lamblike lion feminyne,

> Whose mild meeke propertie aleurth
> This bird to light, and him asseurth.
> (Milligan, 270)

Heywood continues to stress the perfection of such a match: in parentage, dignity, patronage, and benignity they are equally matched. The poem ends with a prayer for a child to unite both the couple and the people of their countries. That the poem is tasteless as well as horrendous must not have been apparent to Mary, for later that year she gave Heywood a grant of lands in Kent and in 1555 reappointed him steward and increased his salary.[31]

But the best indication of Heywood's close relation to Mary —and perhaps with Henry VIII—is preserved by William Cambden. Cambden offers six retorts of our merry wit, two of which offer us exchanges between Heywood and Queen Mary. "When Queen Mary told this Heywood that the Priests must forgo their wives, he merrily answered, 'Your Grace must allow them Lemons then, for the clergy cannot live without sawce.'" "He being asked of the said Queen Mary, what wind blew him to the Court, answered her, 'Two specially the one to see your Majesty'—'We thank you for that,' said Queen Mary; 'but I pray you, what is the other?' 'That your Grace,' said he, 'might see me.'"[32]

In 1556 Heywood finally published his long allegorical poem, *The Spider and the Fly*, the work which he believed to be his *magnum opus*. In it Heywood pays his highest tribute to his Catholic queen by portraying her as the Maid that solves the dispute between the flies (Catholics) and spiders (Protestants) by crushing the spider and sweeping the spider webs from the windows. The ending of the poem, of course, depends upon Mary's gaining the throne; for only then could Heywood bring his poem to a conclusion that satisfied his religious and personal ideas. If Heywood first started the poem around 1536—as he claims in his epilogue—it is then clear that he had been unable to find a satisfactory historical incident with which to end his poem. Mary's accession, with the accompanying return to Catholicism, gave Heywood the historical fact which he only partially turned into allegory.

The next year Heywood penned "A breefe balet touching the traytorous takynge of Scarborow Castell." In April, 1557, Thomas Stafford and his followers captured Scarborough Castle and held it for two days until the Earl of Westmorland recaptured it. A month later Stafford was executed for treason. Heywood capitalized upon this sensational venture to produce a fervently patriotic poem. Besides the light it sheds upon the historical incident, the poem remains an excellent example of the didactic, journalistic ballads of the sixteenth century.

The occasional poem has inherent limitations; for, since both the subject matter and purpose are given, the poet seldom produces poems of any real merit. But Heywood here rises above his other occasional poetry; indeed, the contrast it makes with the fatuous flattery of Mary and Phillip in his marriage poem needs no comment. Heywood addresses the poem to the rebels extolling them for their previous successes, thus emphasizing the stature of this one castle:

> O valiaunt invaders, gallantly gaie,
> Who, with your compeeres, conqueringe the route,
> Castels or towrs, all standynge in your waie,
> Ye take, controlling all estates most stoute.
> Yet had it now bene good to looke aboute:
> Scarborow castel to have let alone,
> And take Scarborow warnynge euerichone.
>
> (Milligan, 272)

The two days that Stafford held the castle are dismissed by a metaphysical argument: "Ye thought ye tooke the castell at your landyng, / The castell takyng you in the selfe whyle." He then switches to the patriotic theme: "A fewe false traytours can not wynne a reame. / Good subiectes be (and will be) trew as steele." "They know gods law; tobey their Kyng and Queene."

Such patriotism and loyalty were well rewarded in 1558. Heywood resigned his position as steward; in return, Mary granted him a lease for forty years of the manor of Bolmer: "Grant of lease for 40 years to John Heywood, of the manor of Bolmer and other lands in Yorkshire, at the rent of 30 £. for his life, and 51 £. 10s. for the rest of the term."[33] We can assume that Heywood resigned the position he had held since 1528 and accepted the grant of lands as possible protection against any reprisals from the Protestant successor. In this way he was no longer dependent upon the public life of the court; perhaps he was anticipating a forced departure later.

But Heywood's fears about Elizabeth were not justified. Of course, he could not have achieved or have held the intimacy with Elizabeth that he had enjoyed with her three predecessors; but it is not true that he was forced into exile immediately upon

Elizabeth's assession. Heywood's exile was a conscious and by no means hasty decision, for a year after Mary's death, Heywood had still some connection with the court:

The v day of August [1559] the Quen['s] grace removyd from Eltham unto Non-shyche, my lord of Arundell['s], and ther her grace had as gret cher evere a nyght, and bankettes; but the sonday at nyght my lord of Arundell['s] howse mad her a grett bankett at ys cost, the wyche kyng Henry the viij byldyd, as ever was sene, for sofer, bankett, and maske, with drumes and flutes and all the mysyke that cold be, tyll mydnyght; and as for chere has nott bene sene nor hard. [On Monday] the Quen['s] grace stod at her standyng [in the further park,] and there was corse^d after; and at nyght the Quen . . . and a play of the chylderyn of Powlles and ther master Se [bastian], master Phelypes, and master Hajwod, and after a grett bankett as [ever was s]ene, with drumes and flutes, and the goodly bankettes [of dishes] costely as ever was sene and gyldyd, tyll iij in mornyng; . . . .[34]

Heywood probably remained in England some five years after Elizabeth gained the throne. A. W. Reed cites a Special Commission Report to prove that John Heywood and his son Ellis left England July 20, 1564.[35] This is the most specific dating available and suggests that Heywood may have supervised the printing of the editions of his works. The title page of the 1561 edition of the *Dialogue of Proverbs* states that the work is "ouersene, and somewhat augmented by the sayde Ihon Heywood." But this claim might well be a printer's false advertisement. Moreover, there is no proof that Heywood watched over the publication of his *Works* in 1562, especially since there were numerous editions of his writings throughout the century.

IV *Heywood in Exile*

In his will—dated and signed from Antwerp in 1564—William Rastell mentions John Heywood, who, we can assume, is alive and in exile, since almost all of the other beneficiaries were exiles. Rastell refers to Heywood thus: "Item do et lego Domino Johanni Heywood, patri dicti Elizei, annulum meum aureum cum effigie capitis mortui cum nomine bonvisi" (Also I give and bequeath to master John Heywood, father of Eliza, my golden ring with the effigy of a decayed head together with the name, Bonvisi.)[36] Bang notes that this ring which Rastell bequeathed to Heywood had belonged to Anthony Bonvisi, a friend of Sir Thomas More.[37] In 1571 Nicholus Sanderus lists Heywood under those "Viri Nobiles ob fidem Catholicam in exilio degentes" (Well-known men in exile because of their Catholicism.)[38]

Heywood's life in exile is poignant. We catch glimpses of a wandering nomad in his last years, an innocent victim of the religious feuding on the Continent. Thomas Wilson, author of the *Arte of Rhetorique*, talked with Heywood at Malines in 1574. It seems that Wilson conveyed to Heywood the Queen's forgiveness and granted him permission to return to England. Wilson writes that he had told Heywood that "the Queen was never so precise that she could not bear with men's weaknesses for their conscience in religion, and only misliked overt acts and rebellious practices."[39] As Bolwell points out,[40] there are interesting implications in this sentence. Did Heywood go into self-exile because of some questionable or treasonable act? Since Heywood had previously been arrested for treason in 1544, it is not unfeasible that he had again been working for a restoration of Catholicism.

Heywood, of course, did not return to England, but spent his remaining years on the Continent. They were not peaceful ones. In 1575 he wrote to Lord Burleigh from Malines a letter that reveals the poignancy of Heywood's last years. Heywood laments his state of poverty, petitions for the income from his various holdings, and predicts his own decease: "And I will god willing your honor shall never heare anie otherwise of me than becometh a poore honest quyett old man, but will spend my tyme, that I have to lyve, in prayer, and in loking to my last ende, whiche cannot be longe, seing my hearing begynneth to fayle me, and my myrth decayeth with age, and my bodie is weake."[41] For some reason Heywood had not received the income from his holdings.

The letter opens with particular stress on his loneliness and his lack of funds:

. . . nowe in my poor old age, when my frendes are in a manner all dead, and manie of them utterlie forsaken me and my wholle lyvyng detayned from me, and the chieffest parte of it, whiche was a lease for years, in Romney Marshe, begged, and bought away utterlie from me; And neither of that, nor of the rest, not one pennye of it, paid, or sent hither unto me, for my maintenance for these twoo yeares, and a half: And (nowe) it pleaseth your good Lordshippe as I heare, to comaund my sonne Doonne, to send me over the arrerages, whiche hath bein deteyned from me, I beseche god reward, and blesse the quenes hignes and your good honor for it.[42]

Heywood's desire to live his last few years in peace was not granted. Father Droeshout has described the experiences of the Catholic community during this tumultuous period. His manuscript—*Historie de la Compagnie de Jesus a Anvers*—contains several references to the Heywood family which D. Stracke, a student of Professor Bang, has summarized. In 1576 John Heywood was admitted to Ellis Heywood's college at Antwerp:

> Le père d'Elisée habitait alors Malines; venu d'Angleterre, persécuté pour la foi, il s'y etait établi. Son fils allait l'y voir pour le consoler. Mais cela le dérangeait dans son travail, c'est pour cela que le P. Mercuriam, général de la Compagnie, autorisa les Pères de la résidence d'Anvers à admettre au Collège avec logement et table séparés le père e'Elisée "ce digne vieillard" "votre vénéré père."[43]

(The father of Ellis lived at that time in Malines; having come from England, where he had been persecuted for the faith, he had there established himself. His son went there to see if he could console him. But this disturbed him in his work; therefore P. Mecuriam, general of the company, authorized the fathers of the residence of Antwerp to admit to the college with separate lodging and table the father of Ellis, "this worthy old man, your revered father.") When the religious conflict came in 1578, the Jesuits attempted to send some of the old fathers to Antwerp. Among this group is John Heywood, who would have been a burden during the riots and battle: ". . . quelques uns des notres qui auraient plus de difficulte a se sauver par la fuite"[44] (some who will have the most difficulty to escape by flight). But supporters of Mathias and the States arrested them at the gates of the city and forced them to return to the college. After the pacification of Ghent, the Jesuits had been forced to swear an oath against Don Juan; they now repudiated this oath and mobs sacked their college and captured all its inhabitants, including John Heywood and his son Ellis (". . . on fait tous les Peres prisonniers et Jean et Elysee avec eux").[45] The Jesuits were to be sent to Malines, but the Duke of Orange planned to send sixty soldiers to kill the Catholics on their way. The Jesuits appealed to Mathias who desired to save them and who sent a guard to protect them on their journey to Malines. He also instructed Don Juan at Louvain to provide protection for them from Malines to Louvain. At Malines the Jesuits met the Franciscans, who had similarly been expelled from Antwerp; and the two groups journeyed on to Louvain: ". . . tous entrent triomphalement a Louvain le 26 mai 1578."[46]

The shock and suffering of Heywood, at this time over eighty years old, must have soon caused his death. We know that Ellis died in October, 1578; and it is doubtful if his father survived him more than a year or so. Witty to the end, Heywood reportedly jested on his deathbed with his confessor, who talked only of the frailty of the flesh: Should I reproach God because he did not make me a fish?[47]

Heywood's family deserves brief mention.[48] Heywood's daughter, Elizabeth, married John Donne and is the mother of the renowned seventeenth-century poet. Two of Heywood's sons, Ellis and Jasper, were the most prominent English Jesuits of the period. Ellis, as I mentioned above, was the companion of his father during the religious turmoil on the Continent. A former secretary of Cardinal Pole, Ellis had exiled himself during Edward's reign and does not seem to have returned to England. At Antwerp, where his father joined him in his own exile, Ellis was spiritual father and preacher.

Jasper Heywood also made an important contribution to English literature by translating three of Seneca's tragedies; *Thyestes*, *Hercules Furens*, and *Troas*. Like his father and brother, Jasper also left England because he could not accept the Protestant reforms. He migrated to Rome where he entered the Jesuit house. He survived his father by some twenty years, and at one time— 1581—traveled to England as a part of a Jesuit mission. He was arrested while in England and was imprisoned without trial until he was exiled to France.

CHAPTER 2

The Non-Dramatic Works

I Dialogue of Proverbs

H EYWOOD'S non-dramatic writings represent the work that
ensured Heywood of his contemporary fame. At first glance,
the modern reader might find them too long and perhaps tedious;
but they should not be disparaged. They reflect both Heywood's
wit and his occasional mastery as a narrator. There are three
specific offerings we must discuss: *The Dialogue of Proverbs,*
The Epigrams, and *The Spider and the Fly.* All of them follow
the extant plays, but no influence of the dramas on these later
works is discernible.

A dialogue conteinyng the nomber in effect of all the prouerbes
in the englishe tongue, compacte in a matter concernyng two
manner of mariages, made and set foorth by Iohn Heywood was
first published in 1546 with subsequent editions in 1549, 1556,
1561; and it was also included in the various editions of his
Works from 1562. The poem is an attempt to include many, but
not all, of the English proverbs in a narrative poem. The attempt
in itself is somewhat of a *tour de force,* and in the past critics
have dismissed the poem as a mere collection. Julian Sharman
wrote: "It cannot be pretended that the volume before us has
other claims to respect besides the extraneous one of its being
the first assemblage of our colloquial sayings."[1] But to dismiss
the poem so summarily is to ignore the structure and characterization that the *Dialogue* offers.

Everyone knows generally what a proverb is, but he might
be hard-pressed to define its salient characteristics. Proverbs
pour from our lips: "April showers bring May flowers," "Look
before you leap," "He who hesitates is lost." Furthermore, we
might know a friend or relative who marshals proverbs for
every argument, every explanation or description. Proverbs do
contain that kernel of truth that such people seek, but obviously

36

as generalizations based on specific instances, they ignore those events which offer contradictory evidence. "He who hesitates is lost" and "Look before you leap" apply to the same event; everything depends upon the point of view. If Darrell and Bill, walking down the street, spy a ten dollar bill on the other side, Darrell might dash across the street. If an automobile hits him, Bill might smugly say as he pocketed the money, "Look before you leap." But a safe dash across the street might prompt a different taunt from Darrell, "He who hesitates is lost." Similarly, a successful joint project lends credence to the proverb "two heads are better than one," whereas a failure of such a project suggests that "too many cooks spoil the broth."

M. P. Tilley offers a concise definition of the proverb which will serve as a starting point: "The typical popular proverb is an old truth concisely and often adroitly worded."[2] But the truth is often a specious one which can be countered by a completely contradictory concept. The poetic characteristics—alliteration, internal rhyme, a certain jingle quality—ensure its popular acceptance. Often the proverb is metaphorical, applying some truth from the animal kingdom to human affairs: "They agreed like two cats in a gutter," "Many a good cow has an evil calf." And often the proverb makes a perceptive and humorous comment upon human conduct or pretensions: "Bachelors' wives and maids' children are well taught." If at times there is a hidden meaning, it is only because the reader is unfamiliar with the references. To be popular the proverb must also be understandable, for it is a means of oral communication. Although Heywood invented some of his proverbs, the proverb is usually the momentary product of a fleeting inspiration; then it was improved and finally petrified by constant use, perhaps preserved for posterity by a Heywood; but it is retained in the colloquial language only as long as its wisdom is relevant; for it is dropped, revised, or replaced as it becomes ambiguous or vague.

Heywood's preface to the *Dialogue* states his reason for writing the poem and his definition of a proverb:

> Among other thinges profytyng in our tong
> Those whiche muche may profyte both olde and yong:
> Suche as on their fruite wyll feede or take holde
> Are our common plaine pithie prouerbes olde.
> Some sence of some of whiche beyng bare and rude:
> Yet to fyne and fruitefull effect they allude.
> And their sentences include so large a reache,

That almost in all thinges good lessons they teache.
This write I not to teache, but to touche: for why,
Men know this as well or better then I.
But this, and this rest, I wryte for this.
Remembryng and consyderyng what the pyth is,
That by remembraunce of these prouerbes maie grow
In this tale, erst talked with a freend, I show
As many of them as we could fytly fynde,
Fallyng to purpose that might fall in minde.
To thentent that the reader redily may
Finde them and minde them, when he wyll alway . . . .

Horace had first suggested that poets desire either to teach
or to give pleasure. By Sir Philip Sidney's time, the poetic
formula for the sixteenth century was to teach and delight.
Heywood here suggests these two goals of literature. Although
he claims to be solely concerned with delight, we can be sure
that his readers saw the poem as a storehouse of wisdom, a
school of proverbial truths.

The importance of the proverb in the sixteenth century can not
be too strongly emphasized. Heywood's poem was a galvanizing
force in its rise in literary esteem; but, even before the publication
of the *Dialogue,* the proverb was a teaching device, a rhetorical
ornament, and a logical support. Erasmus had published his
Adagiorum Chiliades, a collection of Classical proverbs, in 1500;
and the first printed book in England (1477) was Caxton's
publication of *The dictes or sayengis of the philosophhres.* And
in 1542, just four years before the appearance of Heywood's
book, Nicholas Udall published his *Apophthegmes,* another
gathering of proverbs and wise sayings, most of them garnered
from Classical writers or translated from Erasmus, but also
containing some English proverbs.

Rudolph Habenicht has effectively traced the proverb
tradition before it came under Heywood's hand:

Thus, by Heywood's time, the proverb had already been extensively cultivated. It came of age-old tradition rooted in popular
wisdom and morality, exemplified in sacred scriptures of world reli-
gions, and authorized by ancient, medieval, and Renaissance rhetoric
and poetic. It had long served as a pedagogical tool and as a literary
device. It is found in a wide variety of monitary, critical, satiric,
humorous, or serious works, ranging from simple manuals for the
young to some of the chief expressions of literary art.[3]

The proverb gained additional impetus through the publication of Heywood's *Dialogue*. One of the tributaries of the main stream of dramatic literature is the play based upon a popular proverb: *The Longer thou Livest the more Fool thou art; Enough is as Good as a Feast; The Tide tarrieth No Man* (George Wapull, 1576). The purpose of W. Wager's, *The Longer Thou Livest*, printed 1568, is explicit: "A Myrrour very necessarie for youth, and specially for such as are like to come to dignitie and promotion." The hero, the incorrigible Moros, is accompanied through life—and is portrayed in a series of comic scenes—by Idleness, Wrath, and Incontinence. The virtuous counselors—Discipline and Pietie—have no effect upon him since he rejects virtue in all stages of his life. Through Moros' actions we watch the gradual yet inevitable degeneration of a human being—a case study to support the proverb, "The longer thou livest the more fool thou art." Wager's other play, *Enough is as Good as a Feast* (1558-69?) similarly explicates positively and negatively its proverbial title, dividing the cast into good and evil around the protagonist, Worldly Man.

This elaboration of the old morality play into an explication of a popular proverb suggests the popularity and influence of proverbial wisdom in sixteenth-century England. The works of the century abound with these homey sayings; even a casual reading of the Elizabethan dramatists should convince the peruser of their popularity. Shakespeare depends upon them for characterization and for emphasis of a point.[4] Heywood's *Dialogue* of course contributed to this popularity.

Professor Habenicht's introduction to his edition of the *Dialogue* is essential to understanding the various influences upon Heywood's poem. After admirably discussing the proverb collections before Heywood—those of Erasmus, Taverner, Udall, and others—he demonstrates the probable influence of the various sixteenth-century marriage manuals on the choice and handling of Heywood's subject. But "no one source and certainly no one model can account for the complexity of Heywood's *Dialogue*, as no source can be found for the vast majority of his proverbs. Proverbs as a genre and marriage as a topic were both ubiquitous in early sixteenth-century literature."[5]

And actually we must be interested in the poem itself. Anyone who has read either Heywood's *Play of Love* or his *Witty and Witless* is familiar with the form of the poem. Both the debate and dialogue were popular medieval and early Tudor genres,

and the frame of Heywood's poem is in the debate tradition since
the narrator and young lad first present reasons for caution in
marrying and then suggest reasons for haste. The popularity of
the dialogue form in the early part of the century is best
manifested by Thomas More who wrote *Utopia*, his Latin
translations of Lucian, and his reply to Tyndale in this dialogue
form—*A Dialogue Concerning Heresies and Matters of Religion.*

In Heywood's *Dialogue*—divided into two parts with thirteen
chapters in the first part and eleven chapters in the second—the
author creates a persona who tells the story in the first person.
This narrator is visited by a young lad who must choose between
marrying a poor, young beauty or a rich, old, ugly widow. He
seeks the advice of the narrator, prefacing his remarks with a
proverb: "Who so that knew, what wolde be deere, / Should
neede be a marchant but one yeere" (I, i, 8-9). The narrator, who
picks up this proverb, suggests an approach to this dilemma:

> And two thinges I see in you, that shew you wyse,
> First in weddyng ere ye wed, to aske aduyse.
> The seconde, your yeres beyng yong it apeeres,
> Ye regard yet good prouerbes of olde ferne yeeres.
> And as ye grounde your tale vpon one of them,
> Furnishe we this tale with euerychone of them.
> Suche as may fytly fall in mynde to dispose.
>
> (I, ii, 3-9)

The narrator proceeds to marshal for his cause all the proverbs
that caution against haste. The second chapter closes with an
obvious transition; the young lad, who has listened patiently,
rejoins:

> For I agree,
> That those sage sayings dooe weightily way
> Against hast in all thing, but I am at bay.
> By other parables of like weightie weight,
> Which haste me to weddyng, as ye shall here streight.
>
> (I, ii, 58-62)

To see this next chapter as a mere compilation of antithetic
proverbs is to misread Heywood's poem, for the proverbs also
become a vehicle for characterization. The young lad reveals
a certain greed and hypocrisy which are humorous:

> And a thousand folde would it greue me more,
> That she in my foute should die one houre before,

Than one minute after. than haste must prouoke,
Whan the pigge is proferd to holde vp the poke.
(I, iii, 13-16)

Obviously these contradictory proverbs bring about an impasse, so the narrator suggests that the boy list all the advantages that will ensue from the marriage. Again using proverbs, he devotes a chapter to the young girl and one to the rich widow. The narrator sums up the choice: to marry riches without beauty or beauty without riches. Since the proverbs have not helped them reach a decision, the next possibility is the voice of experience, as the narrator has witnessed two marriages that parallel the young lad's choice. A few years before he had had for neighbors a couple that had married for love without money and another that had married for money without love. He proceeds to tell their case histories.

The complexity of Heywod's poem should here be stressed. The lad's seeking advice becomes a frame for two tales which we might well label short stories. But, since the two tales parallel the boy's situation, there is an obvious interconnection between the frame and the inner stories. Moreover, the boy responds to these stories; thus Heywood artistically develops his outer story at the same time he offers two independent, but intertwined tales.

First the narrator relates the bliss of the young couple who had married for love; soon the laughter had turned to moans, and the husband had approached him to lament his state. The narrator suggested that he and his wife visit their relatives, as their parents were dead, to beg a subsistence. The young wife returned first and related her futile trip. Her aunt had refused her request, subjecting her to humiliation and ridicule. Heywood uses the proverbs for comic effect. Our narrator asks, "But where was your vncle whyle all this fray fell? / A sleepe by (quoth she) routyng lyke a hog. / And it is euyll wakyng of a sleepyng dog" (I, x, 192-94).

To avoid the monotony or repetition inherent in the husband's equally futile journey, Heywood introduces several skillful variations. First, the husband does not return until the next day; he had met on the way his uncle's servant ". . . Who gessed streight with this / What mine errand was, offryng in the same, / To do his best for me . . ." (I, xi, 6-8). Staying at the uncle's house is an obnoxious cousin who baits the petitioner. The scene of refusal is handled quickly; the servant and husband depart to try a poorer relative; for, as the servant argues, "Though nought wilbe woon here, I say, yet, ye can / Taste other kinsmen, of whom ye may geat, / Here some and there some, many small make a great" (I, xi, 192-94). Again the proverb is effectively integrated into the conversation.

Heywood then varies this second scene of refusal to avoid repetition; the master of the house is not home.

> To follow his fancy, we went together.
> And toward night yesternight when we came thyther,
> She was within, but he was yet abrode.
> And streight as she sawe me, she swelde lyke a tode.
> Pattryng the diuels Pater noster to hir selfe,
> God neuer made a more croked, crabbed elfe.
> She bad him welcome, but the wurs for mee.
> This knaue comth a beggyng, by me thought shee.
> I smelde hir out, and had hir streight in the wynde.
> She maie abide no beggers of any kynde.
> They be both greedy guts all geuen to get.
> (I, xi, 251-61)

When his kinsman returns, he greets the servant warmly but the young husband coldly; for he immediately realizes the purpose of the visit. Refused again, the two sup and spend the night at an inn; and the servant pays the bill.

The tale of these two young lovers ends in despair. Love is not enough; the landlord demands his rent; there is no food in the house, so the couple separate. The story concluded, the narrator's friend, who sees immediate application to his own plight, wishes to run off to marry the rich widow. The narrator, who cautions him about judging by halves, suggests that they dine so he can continue with his second tale. The young man is further characterized by his actions during the dinner, which Heywood briefly sketches.[6]

> In poste pase we part from potage to cheese,
> And yet this man cride, alas what time we leese.
> He would not let vs pause after our repaste,
> But apart he pluckt me streight, and in all haste . . .
> (II, i, 3-6)

This second tale, which constitutes the second half of the *Dialogue*, is the best part of the poem, for Heywood is at his best in this variation on the May-December marriage. Either he has warmed to his task or the proverbs are more suited to the material, for the tale moves smoothly and skillfully and is very close to being a short story. To add names to the characters would be all that would be necessary to make it one. Moreover, there is a certain Skeltonic quality in the descriptions, as Heywood captures the rough realism that we admire in *The Tunning of Eleanor Rumming*. Heywood deftly describes the bride:

> In this late olde wydow, and than olde new wyfe,
> Age and appetite fell at a stronge stryfe.
> Hir lust was as yonge as hir lymes were olde.
> The daie of hir weddyng, like one to be solde,
> She set out hir selfe in fyne apparell.
> She was made lyke a beere pot, or a barell.
> A croked hooked nose, beetyll browde, blere eyde.
> Many men wishte, for beautifiyng that bryde.
> Hir waiste to be gyrde in, and for a boone grace,
> Some well fauourd vysor, on hir yll fauourd face.
> But with visorlyke visage, suche as it was.
> She smirkt, and she smylde, but so lisped this las,
> That folke might have thought it doone onely alone,
> Of wantonnesse, had not hir teeth beene gone.
> Vpright as a candle standth in a socket,
> Stoode she that daie, so simpre de cocket.
>
> (II, i, 17-32)

The narrator, who was a guest at the dinner at which this couple had its first argument, furnishes us with the intimate details of their dispute; for, from this point he became the confidant of both the wife and the husband. At first they seemed reconciled, but they invited to dinner another couple—the young lovers of the prior tale—and each husband saw in the other's wife the solution to his problem. The one would sacrifice beauty for gold; the other, his ornate plate for that young beauty.

After the dinner episode the narrator serves as the confidant of both the young husband and old wife. Heywood allows each victim of this marriage a chapter to list his complaints (chapters v and vi). Again it is Heywood's comic touch that makes the poem so enjoyable. The widow brags, "To ticke and laughe with me, he hath laufull leeue" (II, v, 167). The narrator comments, "To that I saide nought but laught in my sleeue" (II, v, 168).

Many of the proverbs have a humor in themselves which is
further enhanced by the context. Thus the young husband
compares his boasts before the wedding to his present plight:

> Before I was wedded, and sens, I make recknyng,
> To make my wyfe boow at euery becknyng.
> Bachelers bost, how they will teach their wyves good,
> But many a man speaketh of Robyn hood,
> That neuer shot in his bowe. Whan all is sought,
> Bachelers wiues, and maides children be well tought.
>   (II, vi, 11-16)

But, before the husband can conclude his tale of woe, the
widow returns and interrupts him. We now have a fast-paced
argument between the two, both marshaling proverbs for their
defenses. The exchange is well-handled. When the wife accuses
her husband of lascivious carousing and extravagant spending,
he rejoins with an appropriate proverb:

> And as for yll places, thou sekest me in mo,
> And in woorse to, than I into any go.
> Wherby this prouerbe shewth the in by the weeke.
> No man will an other in the ouen seeke,
> Except that him selfe haue beene there before.
> God geue grace thou hast beene good, I saie no more.
>   (II, vii, 199-204)

In this instance the proverb is effective; it is not a strained
addition to the continuity of the poem, but an excellent, humorous retort to the wife's attack. More examples could be garnered
from this section, for it is the high spot of the poem.

The chapter ends as the widow leaves her husband to his
own devices. The husband, now in a penurious state, has
additional cause to lament. Hopeful of another reconciliation
(since she had kept a bag of money aside), the husband attempts
to woo her again. When he wins her over, she hobbles off
pathetically to fetch her last pittance, which is quickly
squandered. The moral is obvious: "Thus failed all foure, of all
things lesse and more, / Whiche they all, or any of all, maryed
fore" (II, x, 61-62). The young seeker of advice confesses that
he is completely discouraged, but he hopes that individual cases
may not be applicable to himself. He finally decides, however,
to marry neither, since "Who that leaveth surety and leaneth
vnto chaunce, / Whan fooles pype, by auctoritee he maie
daunce" (II, xi, 23-24).

To see this complex poem as a mere collection of proverbs, as Julian Sharman did (see above, note 1), is to do it a gross injustice. Heywood treats the reader to three separate tales or short stories. The characters, most obviously the widow, are well drawn, becoming more than mere stereotypes. There is, especially in the tale of the old widow, sufficient action to ensure a good pace. Although the poem is perhaps a little long and although Heywood occasionally distorts the meaning of the proverb to make a particular point, the *Dialogue of Proverbs* is, on the whole, enjoyable. The proverbs contribute to characterization and action, being essentially well suited to the arguments of these peasant folks.

In the frame story Heywood uses the proverbs mainly for argument; but, once he moves into the inner tales—which are interrelated to the frame story—the proverbs are used for characterization, vivid description, and stimulus to action or rebuttal. The claim on the title page that the *Dialogue* contains all the English proverbs is belied by Heywood's comment in the preface—"In this tale, erst talked with a freend, I show / As many of them as we could fytly fynde, / Fallyng to purpose, that might fall in minde" (14-16); and the final result is a poem in which proverbs are utilized as a means to an end. Heywood is primarily a storyteller, an entertainer, but not just a collector of proverbs.

A few words must be said about the prosody. The poem suffers from obvious faults of the early sixteenth century. Written in couplets with usually ten syllables to the line, the lines have a halting quality that Heywood occasionally overcomes, as in the description of the widow (II, i, 17-64), which moves rapidly and fluently, and is probably Heywood's best sustained passage. The argument between husband and wife is somewhat handicapped by Heywood's continual identification of the speaker, but the exchanges have a liveliness and a flow that demonstrate Heywood's competence in prosody. We do not search through Heywood's poem for poetic gems, but we should demand competent narration. Heywood continually supplies the latter. A passage of this argument should demonstrate Heywood's ability:

> Fewe woords to the wise suffice to be spoken.
> If ye were wise, here were enough (quoth shee)
> Here is enough, and to much, dame (quoth he)
> For though this appeere a proper pulpet peece,

Yet when the fox preacheth, then beware your geese.
A good tale yll tolde, in the tellyng is marde.
So are (quoth she) good tales well tolde, and yll harde.
Thy tales (quoth he) shew long heare, and short wit, wife.
But long be thy legs, and short be thy lyfe.
Pray for your selfe, I am not sicke (quoth she)
Well lets see, what thy last tale comth to (quoth he)
Thou saiest I spend all, to this, thy words wander.
But as deepe drinketh the goose, as the gander.
Thou canst cough in the aumbry, if neede bee,
Whan I shall cough without bread or broth for thee.
Wherby while thou sendst me abrode to spende.
Thou gossepst at home, to meete me at landes ende.
                                                        (II, vii, 150-66)

The interruptions to specify the speaker hinder the flow, but
the rapid give-and-take of the argument comes through. The
Dialogue should not be judged too harshly as poetry. Heywood's
forte is narrative, and in narration he succeeds admirably well.

II   *The Epigrams*

Heywood produced a companion piece to his *Dialogue* in
1555: *Two hundred Epigrammes, upon two hundred prouerbes,
with a thyrde hundred newely added and made by John
Heywood*. In 1550 he had published *An hundred Epigrammes,*
which was reprinted in 1556. *A fourth hundred of Eprigrams*
appeared in 1560, and Heywood added another hundred epigrams, for a grand total of six hundred, when his *Works* appeared
in 1562.[7]

Claim can be made that Heywood's epigrams were the first
ones printed in English; but H. H. Hudson, who emphasizes
the atmosphere that contributed to Heywood's venture into
the form, sees More as the connecting link with the Continent:
"Through his own travels and his friendship with Erasmus he
connects with the great body of European scholars, with whom
epigram writing was a diversion and an accomplishment. And
through quotation, translation, and imitation the influence of
More's epigrams was present in England throughout the
period."[8] More published his *Epigrammata* in 1518.

"Epigram" is an ill-defined term. Originally meaning the
inscription on a monument, the word came to signify any short
poem with some sort of witty turn. Heywood created such epigrams with unbelievable ease. Although some are dull or tedious,

they all manifest a quick mind, a ready wit. Epigram 66 of the *First Hundred of Epigrams* may serve as an example of this wit.

> A widower riche, with riueld face old,
> Wooyng a fayre yong woman, his minde he told.
> Bostyng what he had, as wowers doe, that can,
> Wherein he bosted of a goodly yong man.
> A son of his owne, whome god had him sent,
> Of condicions and qualitees excellent,
> In this whot wooyng this old mans behauour
> So far foorth had won this yong womans fauour,
> That in short tale, whan his long tale was don,
> She prayd him to go home, and send hir his son.

The poem is doggerel; but, as a barb at the January-May marriage theme, it provokes at the least a smile or knowing glance. At his best then, Heywood can turn a fairly polished epigram. Some readers will find much to delight them in Heywood's collection; others will find little. The appeal of the epigram—even more so than that of other comedy or humor—varies from one individual to the other.

It is difficult to appreciate, however, the third epigram in Heywood's initial one hundred. The very definition of the epigram—vague as it is—has been destroyed. Of course Heywood did not concern himself with definition; he would have left that problem to his critics.

Questions answered. 3.

Trust thei any, That trust not many?	} ye.
Please they any, That serue many?	} Nay.
Helpe they any, That helpe not many?	} ye.
Freende they any, That flatter many?	} Nay.
Feare they any, That feare not many?	} ye.
Keepe they any, That keepe to many?	} Nay.

The turn or witty point does not exist. The questions are pseudo-riddles with no humorous appeal. The answers are, of course, obvious.

The witty turn is most apparent in numerous epigrams which feature the exchange of insults or invective. But what might be a witty jab in the context of the argument loses much of its sting on the printed page:

> Were I to wed againe wife, I make a vow,
> I would not wed a wife with a beetill brow.
> And I (quoth she) rather would a husband wed
> With a beetill brow, than with a beetell hed.
>   (I, 79)

One of Heywood's favorite topics is this perpetual argument between husband and wife: "Wyfe, from all euyll, when shalt thou deliuered bee? / Sir, when I (said she) shalbe deliuered from thee" (v, 58).

But Heywood does not limit himself to this subject. He offers six hundred epigrams; and he ranges with similar variation in quality, over much of human experience. One of his most inane epigrams deals with that childhood response of insulting someone with the same epithet he has just used. Heywood sees his example as having an application to other events:

> A man, and his man, chaunced late to bee
> Nie where a crowe stoode criyng in a tree,
> Iames (quoth the maister) the crow hath spyde thee.
> Nay by God, he loketh on you maister (quoth he)
> Taunts (quoth the maister) rebound somtyme I see.
> Where I thought to taunt thee, thou doest taunt mee.
>   (I, 23)

Yet Heywood can move from such an offering to the delightfully ironic "Of dogges and theeues":

> To kepe theeues by night out of my house,
> I kepe dogges to ayde me in my yarde,
> Whose barkyng at stur of euery mouse,
> By lacke of sleepe kylth me in regarde,
> Theeues or dogs than, whiche maie best be sparde?
> Murder is the most mischiefe here to gesse,
> Theeues can do no more, and dogs will do no lesse.
>   (I, 29)

A much longer epigram is "A keper of the commaundementes"; but, since Heywood deals with each commandment separately, the poem may almost be considered as a composite of individual epigrams. It is one of Heywood's best poems and demonstrates brilliantly his satricial powers. The religious hypocrite is unmasked. We should not dismiss it, therefore, as just one of some six hundred epigrams; it is Heywood's masterpiece in the genre:

> If it be (as it is) muche commendable,
> To kepe Gods preceptes, geuen Moyses in table:
> In kepyng the same (as thou hast pretended)
> Thou maist well be marueylously commended.
> First for thy hauyng any mo gods but one,
> Thou kepest within that bound, For God thou hast none,
> Hauyng or worshippyng of god false or true,
> Thou hast nor worshippest God olde nor newe.
> And as for the committyng of Idolatrie,
> By grauyng to thy selfe any Imagerie,
> This twenty yeres daie in weather hot or coole,
> Thou handledst no caruyng nor woorkyng toole.
> The name of God in vayne thou consentst not till,
> Thou neuer swerst but for some purpose good or yll.
> And as for the holy daie, thou doest breake none,
> For thou wilt rather make twentie then breake one.
> Father and mother not dishonoured by thee:
> For thou neuer comst where any of them bee.
> And where thou shalt not kyll, to cleere the of that,
> Thou neuer durst abyde to fyght with a gnat.
> Than all adultery or fornicacion
> Chastitee dischargeth, by this approbacion.
> All women hardly can beare the their fauour,
> To abyde thy sight: and in no wyse thy sauour.
> For stealyng or theft, what euer thou hast beene,
> Thy handes at this daie are knowen to be cleene.
> How canst thou steale ought in house, feeld, or streete?
> Thou sittest in Newgate fast bound handes and feete.
> By false witnesse thou neuer hurtest man, for why,
> Eury woord thou speakest, eury man thinkth a lie.
> Now, to couet in mynde thy neighbours asse,
> Or his house, when bondage will not let the passe.
> To ride to the tone, or go to the tother,
> Or in consented thought one waie or other.
> For to couet thy neighbours maide or his wyfe,
> Thou knowyng, they can not loue the for their lyfe,
> Or of thy neighbours thinges to couet any thyng,
> Whan couetousnes can no way bryng winnyng,
> But that lacke of credite, libertee, or loue,

Kepth the from that couetyng can moue.
Thou hast to shrewde a wit in desyre to dwell,
To haue thinges, from whiche dispeyre doth the expell.
Thus in gods precepts, except thou cleere appeere,
I know not who the diuell can say he is cleere.

(I, 30)

Another favorite device of Heywood is the pun; he bases sixty-eight of his epigrams on puns or verbal quibbles.[9] The pun, of course, is a minor form of verbal wit. There are those who relish the pun whereas others scorn all attempts at such humor. I must leave each reader to his individual judgment, but the following is one of Heywood's best sustained efforts:

Is thy husband a dyar woman? alacke,
Had he no colour to die the on but blacke?
Dieth he oft? ye, to oft when customers call,
But I wolde have him one day, die once for all.
Were he gone, diar woulde I neuer mo wed.
Diars be euer diyng, but neuer ded.

(V, 36)

The most prevalent form of epigram is the one upon a proverb. Heywood offers over three hundred of them, most of them quick two-liners. The quality varies, but Heywood's attitude toward the proverb is similar to the humorous skepticism found in the Dialogue of Proverbs. He delights in poking fun at proverbial wisdom and at those who accept it in complete faith. "Better give then take, all say, but so thinke none: / All thinke better take .XX. poundes, then give one" (III, 11). Heywood adds an important restriction to the cliché that a new broom sweeps clean: "Newe broome swepeth cleane, which is thus vnderstande: / New broome swepeth cleane, in the cleane swepers hande" (III, 67). Another epigram that demonstrates Heywood's perceptive wit is his reply to the proverb, "The greatest clarkes be not the wisest men." He poses the alternative: "Be smaule learnd or vnlerned fooles wysest then" (III, 206). The anti-feminist quality continues in these epigrams upon proverbs: "It hapth in an houre that hapth not in .vii. yeere. / That hapth this houre wife, for thou makst me good cheere" (III, 31).

Taking all of the epigrams in one sitting only emphasizes the tedious quality of many. Heywood occasionally gives several —as many as thirteen—variations on the same proverb. The Epigrams is to be dipped in, to be taken lightly. Heywood is a

genial writer; and, read in the right light, he offers at his best
a humorous insight into human nature and bright laughter over
the foibles and affectations of mankind. His epigrams burst the
balloons of pomposity and pride but do so with little pain. At
times, he is ingenious; at other times, strained; occasionally,
witty; often, dull. But there are enough epigrams that offer
wit and humor to recommend the entire collection. We must
at least smile at Heywood's rendering of a well-known proverb:
"Better one byrde in hande, then ten in the wood. / Better for
byrders, but for byrdes not so good" (III, 40).

As a satirist, he directs his pen against the affectations of
his fellow men. His wit is occasionally sharp, but it is the
general vice, not the individual, that is his victim. His references
to topical events are few,[10] and, although his contemporaries
may have recognized individual people and events in some of
his epigrams, the vast majority have no specific reference.
Typical of his satirical epigrams are these two short offerings,
for which the modern reader must find his own models, as I
imagine Heywood's contemporaries did:

Thy flatteryng of me, this foloweth thervpon:
Other thou are a foole, or els I am one.
Where flattrie aperth, at least: by wyse mens schoole
The flattrer, or the flattred, is a foole.

(I, 73)

He that medleth with all thyng, may shooe the goslyng:
If all such medlers were set to goose shoyng:
No goose neede go barfote betwene this and Greese,
For so: we should haue as many goose shooers as geese.

(III, 199)

And Heywood's tolerant, humane philosophy is best revealed
in a short epigram called "An aduise against mockyng":

Vse to thy true freende no derision
If thy freende spie it, he takth it poyson.
Though thy freende dissemble thespiall cleerely,
Yet spide in a freende it toucheth him neerely.
Tellyng thy freende his faute, mockyng him not,
If he thanke thee not, then is he a sot.

(V, 3)

He refers only occasionally to the Catholic-Protestant problems.
One short poem suggests Heywood's view of the raging
controversy:

> Roome was not bylt on one day, that is well knowne,
> Nor in one Rome wyll not be ouerthrowne.
> For where Rome semd puld downe in one day brother,
> There is Roome set vp agayne in an other.
>
> (III, 274)

The proverb is well known, but Heywood's application of the proverb is not so clear. The Catholic Church had been banished from England by Henry VIII, and Rome seemed pulled down; but, when Mary gained the throne, she restored the Catholic form of worship, and Rome was set up again. The epigram manifests Heywood's joy at Mary's presence on the throne and at what he then thought was the defeat of the Protestant forces.

One epigram Heywood developed from an event in his own life. When a servant in More's house commented upon a guest's long nose and was rebuked, the servant muttered that the man had an attractive nose; after a second rebuke the confused servant cried the man had no nose at all.[11] Heywood tells the story in Epigram 86 of *The First Hundred Epigrams*: "Of the foole and the gentlemans nose":

> One gentilman hauyng an other at meate,
> That guest hauyng a nose deformed foule and great.
> The foole of that house, at this tyme standyng by,
> Fell thus in hand with that nose sodeinly.
>   Nose *autem*, a great nose as euer I sawe.
> His master was wroth, & cride hense with that dawe.
> One saide: talke no more of great noses ye foole,
> Lest ye be talkt withall in the whippyng schoole.
> The foole warnd of great noses no more to speake,
> To mend that faut, this way these woords did breake.
>   Saide I, this is a foule great spittell nose?
> Byr lady I lyed, it is a fayre littell nose.
> Will not that foole be had hence (quoth the master?)
> Thou wilt foole (quoth one) be walkt with a waster,
> If thou speake of any nose, great or small.
> The foole at thyrd warnyng, mindyng to mend all,
> Stept to the boord againe criyng as he gose,
> Before god and man, that man hath no nose.
> The foole was feakt for this: but what of that?
> The great faute here to note, he amended nat:
> Whiche is this: not the wise, but the foole ye see,
> In clokyng of one faute, makth fautes two or three.
>
> (I, 86)

One example of the *fabliau*-type epigram should suffice. I choose this particular epigram because it also handles another of Heywood's important themes—marriage—and reflects Heywood's ingenuity in developing an idea. The reader of his *Dialogue of Proverbs* will remember the dilemma that the young lad faced; at least one boy married the rich widow but did not forgo his beauty:

> Though age and youth together can seeld agree,
> Yet once two yong and two olde folke did I see,
> Agreede lyke lams together dyuers yeres.
> The storie wherof foorthwith aperes.
> A woman olde, and a man young were led,
> She him for loue, and he hir for good to wed.
> A yong woman, and olde man in lyke case,
> Were wed for lyke cause at the same tyme and place.
> Into one house these two couples wedded were,
> And duryng their lyues, together must liue there.
> And they once acquainted, and one month maryed,
> All their liues after they neuer varyed.
> Company and condicion these foure folke hold,
> As nature naturally wylth yong and old;
> Couplyng them seules to gether thus euery daie,
> Tholde fooles aldaie prate, the yong fooles aldaie plaie.

> (I, 33)

There is something in the *Epigrams* for every taste, and it should be occasionally sampled, not just as an historical curosity, but as a testimony to good humor and gentle satire, and as an antidote against pride, pomposity, and pedagogy.

III *Miscellaneous Poems*

I have already mentioned three poems that fit under the classification of miscellaneous: the poem written to Princess Mary, another celebrating the marriage of Mary and Phillip of Spain, and "A breefe balet touching the traytorous takynge of Scarborow Castell." Heywood's reputation cannot rest on the miscellaneous songs and ballads he penned, but such poems deserve at least brief mention. One which borders on an excellent poetic effort is Heywood's early version of Desdemona's haunting song "Sing all a green willow." Heywood occasionally conveys the same charm and beauty; a few verses should establish the tone:

Alas, by what mene may I make ye to know
The vnkyndnes for kyndnes that to me doth growe?
That wone who most kynd loue on me shoold bestow,
Most vnkynd vnkyndnes to me she doth show.
    For all a grene wyllow is my garland.

To haue loue and hold loue, wher loue is so sped,
Oh, delycate foode to the louer so fed.
From loue woon to loue lost wher louers be led,
Oh, desperate dolor, the louer is deade.
    For all a grene wyllow is his garland.

She sayde she dyd loue me and woold loue me still,
She sware aboue all men I had her good wyll.
She sayde and she sware she woold my will fulfill.
The promyse all good, the performans all yll,
    For all a grene wyllow is my garland.

Now wo wurth the Wyllow, and wo wurth the wyght
That wyndyth wyllow, wyllow garland to dyght.
That dole delt in allmys is all amys quyght.
Wher louers are begers for allmys in syght,
    No louer doth beg for the wyllow garland.
                (Milligan, 257-58; ll. 3-22)

Some of the verses falter; Heywood can lapse into such lines as "Lyke the sow of lede on my hed it doth fall. / Breke hed and breke necke, back, bones, brayn, hart, and all, / All partes prest in peces" (ll. 25-27). The alliteration is often excessive, but that is a fault of the age. Such lines as "Now wo wurth the Wyllow, and wo wurth the wyght / That wyndeth wyllow, wyllow garland to dyght" have a flow that demonstrates Heywood's skill. The poem has a certain intensity; it is the bright spot among Heywood's miscellaneous efforts. The poem ends with a fine verse:

All ye that haue had loue and haue my lyke wrong,
My lyke truthe and paciens plante still yow among.
When femynyne fancis for new loue do long,
Old loue can not howld them, new loue is so strong
    For all.
                (ll. 38-42)

The other poems have slight poetic merit, but are most interesting as statements of belief. In "I desyre no number of manye thynges for store," Heywood claims that the grace of

God is the only essential thing in life and exhorts the reader to accept the grace that Christ offers. Several of Heywood's poems discuss such a philosophical or religious theme. "Man, for thyne yll lyfe formerly" urges the sinner to repent and live a virtuous life. The monotonous feminine rhymes are distracting, but the message seems sincere:

> Bere all thyne enmyes quietlye,
> Forgeue thyne enmyes hartelye,
> And axe forgeuenes humblye,
> Where thow offendst offensyuelye.
> Premeditate aduysedly,
> What troobles may fall folowynglye,
> Lest troble towch the terreblye
> By towchyng the to sodenly.
>
> (ll. 25-32, 255)

In another poem dealing with the right way of life—"The harme that groweth of idlenes"—Heywood attacks idleness as the worst of the seven deadly sins:

> As sum one vertu may by grace
> Supresse of vyces many one,
> So thys one vyce, once taken place,
> Distroyeth all vertues eurychone.
> Where this vyce cumth, all vertues ar gone,
> For noe kynd of good busynes
> Can cumpany with idlenes.
>
> (ll. 24-30, 257)

In another poem, "A ballad against slander and detraction," Heywood uses an unusual stanzaic form to vehemently and sincerely lash these vices:

> Then what more ill
> With knyfe to kyll
> Then wyth the toonge to styng?
> With knyfe or toonge,
> Stryke old or yong,
> All in effect one thyng.
>
> (ll. 44-49, 265)

Actually, although the stanza may look unusual, it can be written as a fourteener couplet with internal rhyme:

> Then what more *ill* with knyfe to *kyll* than wyth the
> toonge to styng?

With knyfe or *toonge,* strkye old or *yong,* all in effect
one thyng.

In the first line there are fourteen one-syllable words, and
effect is the only two-syllable word in the stanza. Occasionally
Heywood uses multisyllabic words:

Allmyghty God
Doth shake hys rod
Of iustys on all those
That uniustlye
Detractiuelye
Detract ther freendes or foes.
(ll. 7-12, 263-64)

But each stanza could be printed as fourteeners with an obvious
caesura after the first eight syllables.

And, in one last directive for the good life, Heywood starts a
poem with these two lines: "Man, yf thow mynd heuen to
obtayne, / Bere no males to no wyghte humanyne" (268). He
then details in six stanzas why one should not bear malice to
either friend or foe. The thesis is that God will judge; man
should concern himself with his own well-being to insure
himself of heaven.

Though Heywood wrote several of these directives for the
good life, he never rose above a mediocre level in them. Perhaps
there are inherent limitations in the subject, but Heywood
reveals only a personal inclination for tolerance and restraint,
perhaps a personal fervor, never a poetic one. He is better,
however, in those light, gay songs that might have formed
part of some post-banquet entertainment. "Be merye, frendes,"
and "Ye be wellcum" are two such poems that have this light
sparkle. The opening stanza of "Be merye" is perfectly apt for
after the banquet. The lilting, musical quality of the verse has
an instant appeal, but the message of the poem is actually
serious:

Be merye, frendes, take ye no thowghte.
For worldlye cares, care ye ryght nowghte,
For who so dothe, when all ys sowghte,
Shall see that thowghte auaylethe nowghte.
Be mery, frendes.
(ll. 1-5, 259)

One stanza from this poem perhaps best summarizes Heywood's
life, or at least his attitude:

> Man hardly hath a rycher thyng
> Then honest myrth, the whyche well spryng
> Watryth thee rootes of reioysyng,
> Feedyng the flowers of flooryshynge.
> Be mery, freendes.
>
> (ll. 61-65, 260)

"Ye be wellcum" centers upon an explanation of the greeting, *wellcum* (261-63). Heywood makes a claim for "wellcum" as a better dish than meat; he then separates the components of the word: "What is thys wellcum to tell? / Ye are wellcum, ye are cum well" (ll. 47-48). If one accepts such an interpretation, Heywood's conclusion is obvious. "Your wellcum ys here youre best dyshe" (l. 60). This same type of deft play or turn on words Heywood had perfected in his epigrams. He here toys with another piece of proverbial wisdom: "Welcome is the best cheer" ("cheer" means "dish"). Furthermore, the poem seems well adapted to music. The stanzas move easily, and the people at the banquet could sing along with the poet:

> Where welcum is, thowgh fare be smalle,
> Yet honest hartes be plesde withall.
> Where wellcum wanthe, thowghe grete fare fall,
> No honest hart content it shall
>   Wythout wellcum.
> For honest hartes do euer wyshe
> To haue wellcum to the best dyshe.
>
> (ll. 19-25)

Heywood's extant miscellaneous poems can, in summary, be grouped into four classifications: occasional poetry; love songs; humorous poetry; and philosophical or religious poems. The three occasional poems are one praising Princess Mary, one celebrating her marriage, and a ballad on the Battle of Scarborow Castle. Two of his poems—his version of the willow song and "If loue for loue of long tyme had"—are love songs. Only one poem firmly entrenches itself in the humorous class—"Ye be wellcum." The other poem that I grouped with it above, "Be merye, frendes," is better used as a transition to the largest group of poems, the five philosophical or religious poems: "I desyre no number of manye thynges for store," "Man, for thyne ill lyfe presently," "The harme that groweth of idlenes," "A ballad against slander and detraction," and "Bere no males to no wyghte humayne."

A final poem, "Long haue I bene a singying man," may be
by John Redford; if it is Heywood's work, its autobiographical
character would demand a separate classification. The advocacy
of the middle ground, however, suggests some of Heywood's
other philosophical poems. The first stanza introduces the
extended musical metaphor, through which he argues his point:

> Long haue I bene a singyng man,
> And sondry partes oft haue I soong,
> But one part, sins I fyrst began,
> I cowld nor can syng, old nor yong:
> The meane, I mene, whych part showth well
> Aboue all partes most to excell.
>
> (p. 275)

IV   The Spider and the Fly

Heywood labored meticulously over *The Spider and the Fly*;
it is the work that he expected to be remembered by, but
unfortunately it is a failure. In a poem almost as long as
Paradise Lost, Heywood recounts in rhyme royal an allegorical
tale of a fly caught in a spider's web. It has never been exactly
clear whom the fly and spider represent, but Heywood leaves
no doubt that the maid who rescues the fly and squashes the
spider is Queen Mary. He specifically identifies her in his
epilogue, in which he also states that the poem had lain fallow
for some nineteen years. A lengthy lapse thus exists between
the original plan for the poem and the final stanza.

Before discussing the arguments about the allegorical interpretations, we should first turn to the poem itself. Heywood
prefaces his poem with a short lesson in reading parables. He
tells of three women who are dressing before a mirror. Each is
so envious of the others that she watches them, paying little
attention to herself. The result, of course, is that they are all
ill-dressed, but do not realize it since they are more concerned
with criticizing the one who is absent. Finally, each woman
looks in the glass herself; and, seeing how she is dressed, she
repairs herself. The lesson for the reader of the ensuing allgory
is obvious: Look in the allegory for the reader, not for your
friend: ". . . Which women and glasse, / Are a glasse. this
booke, and readers to compasse."

The opening of the poem attempts to invoke the erotic spirit
of the initial lines of *The Canterbury Tales*:

In season what time euery growing thinge
That ripeth by roote, hath liuely taken hart
Grasse, leafe, and flowre, in field so florishing
That wintered withered stalks, stand in couart
Though weerie wythered harts, plaie than like part
Couertly coucht in bed, them selues to hyde
Yet harts of lust, the bed can not abyde.

(26) [12]

Heywood moves into his subject quickly, relating in the first chapter how, while reading at his desk, he observed the fly falling into the spider's net. The fly laments his state, deploring the fickleness of fortune. Meanwhile, the spider, awakened from his sleep, becomes frightened by the shaking of his cobweb. Relieved to find only a fly, he returns to comfort his family. The spider and the fly then enter into a long argument that is introduced with touches of humor. The spider has granted to the fly the right to speak:

I thanke you humblie (quoth the flie) but sur
Of a goose with garlicke sauste: so late I eete,
That my breath stinketh, and sins I may not stur
From you, for you I thinke it very meete,
To step from me: a loofe: to aire more sweete,
The spider stepping backe a little way,
The flie therwith (somwhat lightned) did say.

(46)

It is in such passages that the true appeal of this poem lies; its mock-heroic aspects are enjoyable. Just as it is inherently humorous for chickens to discuss dreams and free will in Chaucer's "Nun's Priest's Tale," the spider and fly offer a comic tone to the legal quibbling of the day. To be sure, Heywood is basically serious; but the playful wit manifested in his epigrams and proverbs is present here also.

The fly then pleads to have his case heard fairly, a wish that the spider grants, saying he will judge according to reason, law, custom, and conscience. The first part of the poem is obviously a lengthy allegorical satire against the courts and legal practices of the day. The charges and defenses are presented in elaborate detail. Today the reader will find this section dull; the spider and fly chop logic interminably, and then they turn the argument over to their arbiters, the butterfly and ant, who continue the tedious debate.

The first charge advanced by the spider is burglary, a claim that is easily countered. After failing to prove a felony against the fly, the spider asks the fly to prove that he did not come willingly into the web. A long debate over free will and determinism ensues. Finally, the spider changes the charge to trespassing; but the fly again offers an amusing counter anecdote when he compares himself to the driver of a cart who knocks down a house. If the house is off the road, obviously the carter is negligent; but, if the house is in the roadway, the carter is not at fault. Neither is the fly at fault for entering the cobweb, as the cobweb had been built in the fly's roadway. The fly later claims that all holes in windows are the property of flies and that spiders should build by the sides or in the tops. The fly's long legal speech does little to sway the spider for, in one of Heywood's deft comic touches, "But where he thought the spider in study depe, / He was deceiued: the spider was a slepe" (116). The fly, naturally, wishes to repeat his speech; but the spider refuses since his health permits him to sleep but once a day, and there is danger that he may fall asleep again.

Chapter 27 offers an interesting key to the allegory. The spider claims and the fly acquiesces that one can ". . . cowple kynges and peeres, with spiders and flise" (126). Such a passage gives credence to an allegorical identification of the flies with the commons and the spiders with the nobility.

Unable to settle their argument, the fly and spider finally consent to submit their case to arbitration. The fly chooses the butterfly to represent him; the spider appoints the ant. The two disputants separate, each giving a full account of his case to his arbiter. The argument then switches from the fly and the spider to their spokesmen, who hear evidence from the assembled flies and ants. But, even after hearing the evidence on both sides, the arbiters can not agree. Since the evidence seems to be equal, it becomes a question of which side should be believed. The discussion then turns on the honesty of flies and spiders.

Allegorical application of the spider-fly controversy to the tenant-landowner problem of sixteenth-century England is particularly evident in chapter 44, in which the discussion centers around the raising of rents for the windows:

> Fiue foote to two: in windowes of this reme:
> Ye flies hold yet, in lease at unreised rent.

> All holders wherof: sell their wares: as extreme,
> As though their fermes at the most reised rent went.
> Now who beginth here: the first extort extent?
> The flies (quoth the flie) but yet spiders begun:
> To reise rents before: as leases did out run.
>
> (196)

And later in the chapter the fly takes particular issue with
social stratification:

> And yet (I say) in bending our knees to fall:
> Flies looking like lams: spiders lyke lions looke.
> As though poore flies, were made for rich spiders all.
> Of which: though foolish flies: the suffrance may brooke:
> Wise flies can not brooke it: for thei finde in booke:
> This demaund written. When Adam dolue and Eue span,
> Who was in those golden daies, a gentleman.
>
> None as who saie. And were there none now (say wee)
> The worlde shuld be as good now, as it was then.
> If yemen flies: were put in autoritee,
> We wold rule as well, as spiders gentlemen.
>
> (199)

In such passages Heywood's point is clear. The social turmoil
caused by enclosures and exorbitant increases in rent is Heywood's main concern.

The ant and butterfly are unable to reach a decision and
thus call the disputants back to announce that they intend to
leave the argument as they found it. Diplomacy having failed,
the disgruntled flies consider war while the spiders build and
fortify a castle. The illustrations that accompany each chapter
now fill both pages in the battle section, showing graphically
the preparations for war of both camps. The flies capture the
ant and prepare to hang him on the Tree of Reformation. Most
likely Heywood took this detail from the Rebellion of 1549.
Robert Ket, the leader of the rebellion, "hung upon the 'Oak of
Reformation' . . . all country gentlemen who were brought
before him accused of robbing the poor."[13] The ant is, however,
allowed to plead his case. The ant eloquently strikes fear in
the hearts of the flies, and most wish to flee; but the captain
of the flies sees through the ploy and commands him on pain of
death to frighten the spiders similarly. Again the ant is initially
successful, but the captain of the spiders exhorts them to greater
courage. There is now a brief digression as the flies debate the

fate of the ant. Has he fulfilled his task by at least momentarily frightening the spiders or must he die as the flies had formerly decreed? The figurative thumb is turned down, but the ant gains a respite because of several threats from the opposite camp.

When the war finally begins, Heywood describes the onslaught with a certain tongue-in-cheek humor; and the battle sections have an effective mock-heroic quality. A mass of flies darken the sky: ". . . Spider nor flie shrancke, / Hundreds strikin with gonnes, in peeses twentie, / Theare a leg, here an arme, there a head doth flie" (289). During a lull in the battle the spider is petitioned to sue for peace. After the peace terms are arranged, the captain of the flies calls his men together for one last speech before they depart; but only a few attend him. Heywood obviously does not allow his sympathies for the common people to blind him to their shortcomings, for the rude actions of the flies inspire the following exchange:

> How like ye this rudenesse of these flies (quoth he?)
> As yll as anie I have seene (quoth one)
> Well (quoth an other) it is no nouelte:
> Common sort of flies (in maner euerichone)
> As gidds cum and go, so flies cum and are gone.
> Oftimes when strivis are (by wrangling flies) begoon,
> In the mids of the matter, awaie they roon.
>
> (332)

The peace terms are that the flies will have half the holes in the window, but it is not so generous an offer since the spider specifies the smallest holes in the lattice work at the bottom of the window. The fly, at first jubilant at the prospect of half the area of the window, is dismayed with, but resigned to, the terms.

Next the fly and spider change places, since the spider claims that the fly would see things correctly if he could make such an exchange. In a humorous little digression, the fly puffs out with arrogance and claims all of the window for the spiders. He soon realizes his slip and begs the spider to disregard such a rash statement—this passage is difficult to correlate with any specific historical event, for the peasants or common people were never placed in such a position, and it is not until Mary gains the throne that the Catholics are in power. It is more likely that Heywood is here satirizing human pride and conceit. As one close to both the throne of Henry VIII and Edward VI, he was not in complete sympathy with the peasants nor totally alienated from the nobles.

Finally, the spider concludes that, on the grounds of reason, law, custom, and conscience, the fly must die. He is about to execute the fly when the maid enters the room, strikes down the cobweb, and prepares to kill the spider, who now finds himself pleading for life. She promises to hear him just as he listened to the fly. The result is similar but, thankfully, is reached more quickly. Before the spider dies, he is granted permission to speak to his family, whom he instructs in the right type of living. I think that there is little doubt that the Spider here represents Archbishop Cranmer who was executed by Mary on March 21, 1556. Cranmer also recanted, although the night before his death he repudiated his former recantation—a fact that Heywood ignores in his poem. Northumberland had also recanted before his death in 1553, but the lapse of three years between his execution and the publication of Heywood's poem is not easily explained. Cranmer's recent death would have been on the reader's mind.

After killing the spider, the maid summons twelve spiders and twelve flies and lectures them on the dangers of "misorder" and exhorts them to "grow to order":

> But leaue this, and take that: mine order erst told.
> Keepe you your places, and let me keepe mine.
> As nature: and custom: willeth you of old.
> While reason: and custom: do me cleere encline:
> My masters and maistres will: to woork in fine:
> As I under them: and you under me,
> May louelie liue (I saie) ech in dew degree.
>
> (415-16)

In an epilogue Heywood details parts of the allegorical application: "Ye se also: that this fygure here implies, / For strife in windowes: betweene spiders and flies. / The plat of all the world, and people therin" (424). And he sings hymns of praise to Queen Mary:

> To our sufferaigne Ladie, Queene Marie, and maide.
> At gods bringing whom to her crowne, may be laide:
> Our lyke strife rissen: and more then like to rise,
> Then showth here risen: betweene spiders and flies.
> Whose sworde like a brome: that swepth out filth cleane:
> Not a sword that filith the house: by blodie meane,

This mercifull maiden tooke in hand to sweepe,
Her window: this realme. Not to kill, but to keepe:
All in quiet.

(426)

The poem, however, is too long. Heywood is not skillful
enough as a poet to meet the demands of rhyme royal over an
extended period. The allegory of the poem is too confused to
attract the average reader; and, if we can judge from contemporary reaction, Heywood's hopes for what he considered his
magnum opus were misguided. William Harrison comments
upon Heywood's poem in his "Description of England," which
was included in Holinshed's *Chronicles*: "One hath made a
booke of the *Spider and the Flie*, wherein he dealeth so
profoundlie, and beyond all measure of skill, that neither he
himself that made it, neither anie one that readeth it, can
reach into the meaning thereof."[14]

At one level, of course, *The Spider and the Fly* is a religious
allegory, the flies representing the Catholics, the Spiders the
Protestants. But such an identification is valid only for the
last few chapters and is misleading for the early part of the
poem. If we move back twenty years from the date of publication, we may better search for a key to the allegory. Since
Heywood himself claimed that the idea for the poem originated
twenty years prior to the date of publication, the events in the
early 1530's—a period of turmoil—may offer some clues to the
poem's meaning. The divorce question, the fall of Wolsey, and
the imprisonment and execution of Thomas More would have
concerned Heywood. Perhaps the Pilgrimage of Grace might
have attracted Heywood's attention, although it is impossible
to find one event in this period which fits all of the circum-
stances of the poem. But the Pilgrimage of Grace offers a
religious uprising, a peasant revolt, that could be handled
allegorically. But the spiders must then also represent the noble,
landed class, which was mainly Protestant and the flies, the
peasants, who were for the most part Catholic. It seems clear
from reading the poem that it is primarily the plight of the
common man that affected Heywood. The religious factor seems
secondary.

There were other economic and religious uprisings that could
as easily have served as the inspiration for the battle between
the spiders and the flies. Robert Ket, a tanner and landowner,

led a rebellion in 1549 to protest the enclosures in Norfolk. This rebellion, known as "Ket's Rebellion," was economic in origin, although the separation of Catholic peasant and Protestant nobility still would have afforded Heywood an important motif. Ket can be advanced as an interesting candidate for the Fly; but again the revolt was abortive, and Heywood would have had no ending for his poem.

David Hauser offers still another incident for the allegorical basis: "The battle between the spiders and the flies which takes place in Chapter 66 represents neither the Pilgrimage of Grace nor the Rebellion of 1549, but an uprising nearer 1555."[15] Whereas all other interpretations must deal with the problem of Heywood's intentions around 1530 and his final poem in 1556, Hauser argues for a strict unity in the poem, a unity that he alone recognizes: "The concept of rebellion had been so heavily emphasized that it was ideally suited to convey connotations of injustice, social inequality, and instability. Looking at the poem in this light, we find, not a lack of unity among parts as some critics have maintained, but a continuous dramatic portrayal of the failures of the law courts, the economic grievances of agricultural workers, and the lack of any real temporal or spiritual authority."[16]

If there is little agreement about a particular historical incident inspiring this long poem, the allegorical intent of the ending is fairly clear. Heywood himself tells us that the maid is Queen Mary. The Spider is most likely Archbishop Cranmer who was executed in 1556. Lord Northumberland is another possible candidate, but his death in 1553 would not have had the contemporary significance that Archbishop Cranmer's more recent death had. But Cranmer can not be the Spider in the early chapters if the poem was first conceived in the early 1530's. Jakob Haber has discussed the poem in the most detail and in his summary of the allegory he attempts to pinpoint the changes in Heywood's allegory.

In the first part (chapters 1-27) the spiderweb represents, says Haber, the laws; the spider, the judge, or Cardinal Wolsey; the fly, the peasants and tradesmen, the "commons," who are at the mercy of the arbitrary actions of the judges. In the second part, which was written much later, the flies represent the commoners, as they did in the first part; the spiders, however, are now the great landowners; and the spiderweb, their landed property which they have expanded unduly. They have banished the yeoman-flies from their farms through sundry dodges, mainly through exorbitant increases in the rents for the farms. The battle is modeled closely upon the incidents from 1549 to 1553. The Spider is here the Duke of Northumberland, the Maid with the Broom is Queen Mary, and the Ant is probably to be understood as the clergy which played a mediating role."[17]

There is no need to question Haber's claim that Heywood's poem reflects the social turmoil of the period. Haber quotes extensively from contemporary sources to prove that this constant struggle over rents and enclosures between the landowner and peasants was a concern of many writers of the age.[18] When we turn to the identification of the fly and spider, however, agreement is not so easily reached. If, in the first part of the poem, the Spider represents Wolsey, then the original inspiration for the poem must be pushed back even further; Wolsey, who fell from power in 1529 and died in 1530, would no longer be a suitable figure for a satirical allegory.

Bolwell suggests, however, that the Fly may represent Sir Thomas More, ". . . caught in the web of Henry VIII and the plottings of his queen. The web was wrongfully placed in a free area; if the web were in its rightful place the Fly would not have been caught. So if Henry had not defied the Church and worked unlawfully with Anne Boleyn, More would not have been caught."[19] Bolwell's suggestion is interesting. Surely the Fly's insistence that he has freedom of conscience suggests both More's and Fisher's insistence on liberty of conscience. Since there was no ill will in their hearts, they were not guilty as accused. Also, if More is the Fly, the Spider is not Wolsey but perhaps Cranmer, or Thomas Cromwell who rose to a position of power after Wolsey's fall.

This survey of possible identifications should demonstrate the problems of the poem. It is not a unified effort, and the continual speculation bears little fruit. It is impossible to prove that the Pilgrimage of Grace is the source for the battle between the flies and spiders. Heywood does not mention the various demands of the Pilgrimage, such as the insistence on the restoration of the monasteries or repeal of the Statute of Uses. It is only clear that the poem discusses allegorically the civil strife and the dissension of the period. Perhaps the meaning of the poem is more general than is normally maintained. R. J.

Schoeck in an article in *Notes and Queries* has offered the following possible source for Heywood's poem; a quotation from Plutarch in Chapter Six of Erasmus's *The Education of a Christian Prince*: "Nothing should be more democratic or just than the prince; so with the law. Under any other conditions you will have the situation which the Greek philosopher well stated: "Laws are merely spider webs, which the birds, being larger, break through with ease, while the flies are caught fast."[20] Perhaps the poem can best be read in terms of Heywood's general reaction to the injustices and inequities of the period.

Through the allegory, however, moves one important theme, a theme made explicit in the last few chapters: The need for order as a control on chaotic existence; the necessity of proper rule and loyal obeisance; the necessity of strong but just rule —these motifs attract the student of Tudor cultural and political history, if not the lover of literature. Perhaps finally, the poem is best left unread except by the cultural historian.

For though the poem has historical interest, it has little esthetic merit. The major fault is that no clear plan controlled the work from its inception. The conclusion depended upon Mary's gaining the throne, a possibility that Heywood could not have had in mind when he first began. The problem is that neither the reader today nor Heywood's contemporaries could penetrate the allegory. It is evident that a concrete, historical personage exists behind the Spider; but Wolsey, Cromwell, Cranmer, and Northumberland all offer themselves as candidates.

The poem does mark, however, a significant departure from the medieval tradition. Heywood does not deal with vague abstractions or personifications but presents real political figures under the guise of allegory. There is a distinct difference between Stephen Hawes's *The Pastime of Pleasure* and Heywood's *The Spider and the Fly*.

The Spider and the Fly does represent, moreover, the ideas and philosophy of the More circle. The same spirit that moved Thomas More to write *Utopia* must have been responsible for such a social document as *The Spider and the Fly*. Both works are concerned with social conditions in England, and both suggest possible solutions. Here John Heywood reflects that humanistic background to which he was exposed during his years under More's influence both at his home and at Henry

VIII's court. Jakob Haber has best described the relationship
between More's philosophy and Heywood's poem. Heywood is
not a philosopher who constructed a system of political life
as More did; he is a practical man who proceeds from that
which exists and attempts to improve it, whereas Thomas More
produces something completely new. The administering of
justice and landed property, as well as the system of government
are Heywood's themes; More deals not only with these questions
but also with many others.[21]

The Spider and the Fly, alone of Heywood's works, can be
squeezed among the shelves of humanistic books of the first
part of the sixteenth century. Its religious bias does not detract
from its social concern; Heywood is never so biased that he
can not satirize the pretensions and faults of both sides. The
poem also manifests, therefore, the tolerance that is Heywood's
most attractive trait.

CHAPTER 3

The Dramatic Works

I The Heywood Canon

THE Heywood canon of dramatic works divides into two groups, the so-called debates and the farces. To the first category belong *Witty and Witless, Love,* and *Weather;* to the second, *The Four PP, The Pardoner and the Friar,* and *Johan Johan.*[1] Arguments for his having written *Gentleness and Nobility* have been most effectively advanced by Kenneth W. Cameron. On the other hand, Charles W. Wallace has claimed that it is unlikely that Heywood was the author of any of the farces and has suggested William Cornish as the real author.[2] Because there is some question about the authorship of the three farces, a brief survey of the external evidence for Heywood's authorship is necessary.

To answer Wallace's very subjective claims is difficult, for he states that *The Pardoner and the Friar* is "commonly attributed to Heywood because no one else seemed to be in sight to father it upon."[3] Wallace's candidate, of course, is Cornish; and after he discusses his authorship of *The Pardoner and the Friar* and *The Four PP,* he turns to *Johan Johan.* His main argument for Cornish's authorship of *Johan Johan* is that he is the "only man who was writing this sort of play."[4] To read Wallace is to gain the impression that Cornish was the only dramatist of the period: "While we are about it, we may observe that no other dramatist than Cornish was then living who had either opportunity or impetus or skill to write in the manner of his new-style drama three other plays, namely, *Of Gentleness and Nobility,* likewise ascribed by some to Heywood, *The Four Elements* (composed c. 1517-20), and *Calisto and Meliboea,* the first English version of the Spanish tale that was then taking all Europe by storm."[5] Wallace also attacks the idea that a loyal Catholic such as Heywood could have satirized the church as the author of the three farces did.

These plays were not included when Heywood's *Works* were published in 1562. In 1619 John Pitseus (*Relationum Historicarum de Rebus Anglicis*) mentions the three plays that Bishop Bale (*Scriptorum illustriu Maioris Brytannie . . . .*) had included in his list of Heywood's works in 1557: "De quadruplici (P)," "De aura comediam," and "De amore tragoediam." Thus *The Four PP, Weather,* and *Love,* which is curiously referred to as a tragedy, have the questionable authority of contemporary testimony. More important, William Rastell, Heywood's brother-in-law, printed *Love* and *Weather* in 1533 with Heywood's name on the title pages. William Middleton (who printed from 1541 until his death in 1547)[6] printed *The Four PP* with an undated title page that claims that the play was "made by John Heywood."

Could Middleton either have made a mistake or have purposely assigned an anonymous play to Heywood? Since the play was written in the 1520's, the late publication date presents some difficulties. There may have been an earlier edition, of which no trace remains; the play was surely available when Rastell was printing other Heywood plays; and both William Copland and John Allde published the play again before 1570. We can not be positive that Middleton is the first publisher; he may have attempted to capitalize on the prominence of Heywood's name around 1544 by republishing the play.

Despite Wallace's comment about Heywood's Catholicism, such a satire about Catholic clerics as we find in *The Four PP* could not have hurt Heywood's cause when he was being accused of treason. In 1544 he had renounced the supremacy of the Pope and had accepted the Henrican doctrines. His satire against the pretensions of two clerical figures—the palmer and the pardoner—would gain a more topical interest around this period. Nothing in *The Four PP*, on the other hand, supports the conjecture that Middleton has added Heywood's name to an anonymous play.

Witty and Witless was never published during Heywood's life, remaining in manuscript until F. W. Fairholt edited the play in 1846. The original manuscript closes with the inscription "Amen qd John Heywood." Such contemporary evidence does not exist, however, for *The Pardoner and the Friar* (1533) and for *Johan Johan* (1533),[7] the best of these six plays. Francis Kirkman in 1671 first assigned these plays to the Heywood canon. William Rastell, however, had published them anonymously.

On the basis of external evidence then, we can definitely assign *The Four PP, Weather, Love,* and *Witty and Witless* to Heywood. But when we discuss the plays, we must seek internal evidence to confirm the usual assignment of *The Pardoner and the Friar* and *Johan Johan* to John Heywood. I will first treat these six plays as dramatic works of art and turn to the problem of Heywood's sources in a subsequent chapter.

II *The Debates*

Of the six, *Witty and Witless*[8] is the dullest. It may very well be the earliest of Heywood's plays, although the order of composition is extremely difficult to determine. In any case, it is a play only because it fits the most general definition of the term. If imitation and complete dependence upon dialogue are the only two essentials of drama, then *Witty and Witless* fits the definition. Three actors take parts; and the action, using this term in a very loose sense, advances entirely by dialogue. Except for the brief changeover in the middle of the play, there are only the two debaters on the stage at any one time. Moreover, the actors could easily have read their parts from podiums on opposite sides of the stage, for the dialogue suggests no comic action which we come to expect in such later plays as the anonymous *Thersites* and Thomas Preston's *Cambises.* If *Witty* was a humorous play in its time, it offers a certain test to any claim about the universality of humor or of the comic muse.

The first few lines are missing from the manuscript, but no reader laments the loss, probably feeling that the some 850 lines are enough. John, the advocate of wit, who unfortunately is rather dull, is engaged in debate with James, who claims it is better to be a fool—a witless person. James first argues that, since the fool doesn't have to work, he avoids the pain of labor while still obtaining the necessities of life. But John is at his best in the first part of the debate as he claims that wise men beat fools. His description of the sundry methods of beat-

ing that fools are subject to indicate the quality of Heywood's
Skeltonics:

> Some beat hym some bob hym
> Some joll hym some job hym
> Some tugg hym by the hers
> Some lugg hym by the eares
> Some spet at hym some spurne hym
> Some toss hym some turne hym
> Some snap hym some scratch hym
> Some cramp hym some cratch hym
> Some cuff [hym] some clowt hym
> Some lashe him some lowte hym
> Some whyske hym some whype hym
> Wythe scharpe naylys some nype hym.
>
> (118)

John thus wins the first point by proving that fools have pain,
whereas "The wytty who beate them selves by bysynes / May
oft yn beatyngs favowr them selves I ges" (121). But, since both
suffer pain, James argues that one might as well be witless as
witty. John's reply manifests the stilted quality of the dialogue;
for Heywood's early plays abound with word worrying, puns,
strained alliteration, and the language of the court or intellectual circles:

> That conclewsyon ys conclewdyd wysely
> Your pryme proposycyon dyd put presysely
> Better to be wyttles then wytty and now
> As good to be wyttles as wytty sey yow
> But that wytt whych putth case in degre comparatyve
> And conclewdyth case in degre posytyve
> Sall not in that case clame degre sewperlatyve.
>
> (122-23)

And a few lines later, John uses a variation of *say* eight times
in four lines:

> Ye sey so and seyd so but so seyd not I
> Nor sey yt not yet but that seyng deny
> And tyll sayng prove y[our] sayng more playnely
> I wyll asay to sey the contrary.
>
> (123)

Such dialogue does not appeal to the modern reader, but the
audience of *Witty* and *Love* must have enjoyed such verbal
juggling as an ornament to the debate itself.

But the direction of the debate turns rapidly; for James, who one must admit is "wittier" than his opponent, argues that the labor of the mind is more painful than physical labor. When he offers for comparison the student and the laborer, John agees that the witless cannot suffer from this pain of the mind and grants that the witty must therefore have greater pain. In a desperate attempt to reverse the flow of the argument, John advances the theory that the witty will have greater pleasures, those of the mind. But even this claim is countered by James, who insists on salvation as the greatest pleasure, an end which is only guaranteed the witless. The witty will be saved *if* they do well; but, as James emphasizes, this is a big "if." A witless person, who can not be held responsible for his actions, can rest assured that he will gain salvation, just as the baptized child who has not yet gained the age of reason is saved. John concedes; he grants that it is obviously better to be witless than witty.

The first part of the little drama now over, a third character, Jerome, enters; and, after a brief exchange, James exits. Jerome, who has the task of reconverting John to the side of wisdom and intellect, first makes an important distinction between the wise and the witty. It is possible to be witty without being wise, but there can be no wisdom without wit. Thus the audience sees Jerome as the wise man with an ample supply of wit and James as one who is witty without being wise. John, at least in the early part of the play, has neither wit nor wisdom.

Jerome then poses the question upon which the rest of the argument hinges: Would you rather be a reasonable man or an unreasonable beast? The question is a commonplace; the answer is obvious. After Jerome has equated the fool with the beast, John is brought one step closer to his conversion. The last crux is the question of salvation, of which the fool is assured. Jerome argues that the better the life on earth, the better the reward in heaven. John is still reluctant, for the witty one takes a chance; he questions Jerome with a proverb —"Better one bird in hand than ten in the woods"—but Jerome says that the wise man will risk the loss since he has such an excellent opportunity to catch all ten. John, now convinced of his former folly, completely embraces Jerome's ideas.

The play ends with four stanzas of rhyme royal, the first three of which are to be presented only if the king is in the audience.

Heywood is able to turn the theme of the play into a compliment
to Henry VIII, "owr most loved and drade supreme soferayne /
The shynyng of whose most excellent talent / Imployde to gods
glory above all the trayne / Thus wytt wantyth her recytall to
retayne" (142). There may be a reference in this courtly
compliment to Henry's *Assertio Septem Sacramentorum,* which
he had written by May, 1520, and for which the Pope bestowed
the title *Fidei Defensor* on Henry in October.

A secondary purpose of the play—to attack Will Summers, the
king's jester—is evident from several references to him. Early
in the play, when John describes how fools are beaten, he cites
one specific fool: "Not evyn mayster somer the kyngs g[r]acys
foole / But tastythe some tyme some nyps of new schoole" (118).
Jerome later uses Summers as an example:

> Then shall thes beasts wyttles man and mylhors draw on
> Bothe yn one yok for thynk yow the nombere
> Standth as somer dothe all day yn slomber
> Nay somer ys a sot foole for a kyng
> But sots in many other mens howsyng
> Bear water bear woodd and do yn drugery
> In kychyn cole howse and in the nersery.
>
> (136)

Where formerly John had thought it better to be "sot somer
then sage salamon," at the end of the play he realizes that it is
better to be "sage salaman." Thus Heywood not only presents
an entertaining debate for his audience, which included Henry
VIII; but he also attacks one of his rivals for the king's favor.
The epilogue also states, "As scryptur alegyd late doth wytnes
/ The wytty wyse wurker to be prefarde / Above thydyll
sott . . ." (143). The audience could hardly miss the topical
allusions to the professional rivalry between the hard-working
court entertainer, Heywood, and the idle fool, Summers.

Yet these allusions are surely only secondary. The debate
is a part of the humanistic tradition or more specifically of the
fool literature such as Erasmus' *Encomium Moriae* or what is
often termed the play's source, the French *Dyalogue du fol et
du sage, a debat.*[9] One passage from Erasmus should demonstrate
the similarity of Folly's ideas with the arguments of James:

Let me return to the topic of the happiness of fools. After a life
lived out in much jollity, with no fear of death, or sense of it, they
go straight to the Elysian Fields, there to entertain the pious and

idle shades with their jests. Let us go about, then, and compare the lot of the wise man with that of the fool. Fancy some pattern of wisdom to put up against him, a man who wore out his whole boyhood and youth in pursuing the learned disciplines. He wasted the pleasantest time of life in unintermitted watchings, cares, and studies; and through the remaining part of it he never tasted so much as a little of pleasure; always frugal, impecunious, sad, austere; unfair and strict toward himself, morose and unamiable to others. . . .[10]

Although I would not argue for any direct source, the arguments of James are surely reflected in such a passage. The thinking of the More circle is most likely the motivating force behind the debate and especially the addition of Jerome. The distinction between man and beast that Jerome makes is as old as Aristotle, and his emphasis upon salvation through deeds is a direct reflection of the Catholic theory of good works.

Before Heywood wrote his debates or dialogues, the genre was non-dramatic. Although Heywood casts his debate in the form of a drama, he does not take advantage of the dramatic form. *Witty and Witless* remains basically undramatic; it remains a curious manifestation of a particular taste in early Tudor England. Although *Witty and Witless*, merely a debate, offers no dramatic conflict, no action, and no character development, the play, as a part of the literature of folly, dramatizes Tudor concepts of intellect. Heywood is attempting to entertain a sophisticated audience with current ideas dressed in a palatable form; he suggests nothing new or startling in the play. Whether or not *Witty* is Heywood's first effort is, of course, debatable; but there is a marked difference between *Witty*, *Love*, and *Weather*. As drama, *Weather* is far superior to the first two; and *Love* shows a keener sense of both character and dramatic conflict than *Witty*.

Love is still a disputation, but the reader now recognizes a controlling structure, dramatic conflict and physical action. *Love* is not only tolerable, but quite often actually entertaining. The four characters in the play represent all aspects of love: Lover-loved; Lover-not-beloved; Neither-lover-nor-loved; Beloved-not-loving (a woman). Neither-lover-nor-loved is the vice character or villain who delights in the plights of his opponent, Lover-loved.

The play opens with Lover-not-beloved lamenting his state: "Of all paynes the most incomparable payne / Is to be a louer

not louyd agayne" (ll. 62-63). Beloved-not-loving enters immediately to dispute this point, and the first of the debates is under
way:

> Then standyth our question betwene these twayne
> Of louing not louyd, or louyd not louing
> Which is the case most paynfull in sufferyng
> Wherto I saye that the most payne doth moue
> To those belouyd of whome they can not loue.
>
> (ll. 80-84)

Since neither is able to convince the other, they exit after
deciding to submit their case to arbitration. Lover-loved
immediately enters the empty stage "with a songe" and
ecstatically recalls his pleasure. His disputant is Neither-lover-
nor-loved. After failing to reach any agreement, Lover-loved
exits. In a long speech to the audience Neither-lover-nor-loved
relates an experience which made him such a cynic. He had
once feigned to love a beautiful young lady whom he humorously
describes in rapid-fire couplets which, except for the absence
of sustained rhymes, we call "skeltonics."

Neither-lover-nor-loved was a practical man, as he indicates
in this passage: "We parted and I the nexte morne dyd aryse /
In tyme not to tymely such tyme as I coulde / I alowe no loue
where slepe is not alowde" (504-6). A distinct personality
emerges, making this one character very engaging; the contrast
with the ideal, sentimentalized Lover-loved becomes more than
a contrast of types. In this long soliloquy Heywood gives
Neither-lover-nor-loved a believable and entertaining basis for
the stereotyped cynicism suggested by his name.

The scene is for actor and audience, and the reader has to
visualize for himself the actions and innuendoes that would have
made the performance so entertaining. To hold the stage for 291
lines is difficult, but Neither-lover-nor-loved commands attention. First, he denies that he had any feeling for his loved one
except the pleasure he might obtain from a contest of wits. He
insists that he feigned being a lover, and was never such a fool
as to fall in love. Since a vice-character supposedly needs no
motivation, Heywood could have eliminated this monologue; but,
by including it, Heywood gains a certain muddled but believable
motivation for him. Neither-lover-nor-loved is more than a vice
or mere abstraction, and the tale he relates is more than a gra-
tuitous *fabliau*. He scorns the sentimental lover because of his

own experience, and it is only when the vice achieves such motivation that he becomes artistically defensible. In this one character, Heywood makes that important move from abstraction to individual.

Continually claiming that he was only pretending to love her, Neither-lover-nor-loved describes his plot to terminate his affair. One passage in particular demonstrates that we are listening to an individual, not to a type:

> And I to shewe my selfe in lyke louyng
> Dissimiled lyke chere in all her lyke lokyng
> By this and other lyke thynges then in hande
> I gaue her mockes me thought aboue a thousand
> Wherby I thought her owne tale lyke a bur
> Stack to her owne back mockum moccabitur
> And vpon this I fell in deuysyng
> To brynge to ende this ydell disgysyng
> Wherupon sodaynly I stale away
> And when I had ben absent halfe a day
> My harte mysgaue me by god that bought me
> That yf she myst me where I thought she sought me
> She sewer wolde be madde by loue that she oughte me
> Wherin not loue, but pety so wrought me
> That to returne anone I bethought me.
>
> (ll. 597-611)

Surely we can penetrate the cynic's mask and recognize that his cynicism results from his own experience. Although the play presents Neither-lover-nor-loved after this incident, what he was like before this affair is a moot question; but Heywood offers an amusing rationalization for his subsequent actions.

When Neither-lover-nor-loved returns, a waiting woman reports that his mistress has died of grief. Prevented from entering the house, Neither-lover-nor-loved is honestly distraught:

> I standyng without halfe out of my wyt
> In that this woman sholde dye in my faute
> But syns I coulde in there by none assawte
> To her chamber wyndowe I gat about
> To see at the last way the cors layd out
> And there lokyng in by godes blessyd mother
> I saw her naked a bed with an other.
>
> (ll. 620-626)

Neither-lover-nor-loved next relates an exchange between himself and his former mistress; she claims that she had perceived from the beginning that he was merely trying to mock her and thus she had also been playing the part of the lover.

Heywood here makes an important step in dramatic technique between these two plays—*Witty* and *Love*. Without this soliloquy, however, the advance is by no means so apparent, although adding a fourth character and paralleling the conflicts are in themselves striking additions. The *fabliau*-like tale has an important role in the development of a character; it is not a mere digression. Neither-lover-nor-loved is a motivated character. No vice or abstraction returns for pity's sake or sorrows over a victim's death; the cynic may have done both and now rationalizing his actions, claims he has learned his lesson.

After this explanation to the audience, the other disputants return to engage in some slapstick humor. It should be easy to visualize the stage action in the following passage as Neither-lover-nor-loved hops back and forth, creating confusion and a low humor:

> Ye haue ben here before me before now
> And now I am here before you
> And now I am here behynde ye
> And now ye be here behynde me
> And now we be here euyn both to gether.
>   (ll. 703-7)

Each pair of lovers then asks the other to arbitrate its dispute. Lover-not-beloved and Beloved-not-loving first debate on which has the greatest pain. Merely to state that one suffers pain proves nothing, for the question is one of degree. What interests us is the argument by analogy; Lover-not-beloved poses this question: "A man that is hanged or that mans hangman / Whiche man of those twayne suffereth most payne?" (ll. 884-85). Since none can deny that the one hanged suffers pain, Lover-not-beloved claims victory as he is analogous to the hanged man. Yet our heroine twists the argument nicely: "But of those at whose hangyng haue hangman by / Howe many haue ye knowen hang wyllyngly?" (ll. 895-96). Similarly she claims that she is loved against her will; she is powerless, whereas Lover-not-beloved by an effort of will can eliminate his travail.

Before judgment is passed, Lover-loved and Neither-lover-nor-loved present their arguments. The initial phase centers around which state has more pleasure, and then the argument turns into a discussion of the relationship of pleasure and contentment.

Lover-loved claims that "Pleasure without contentacyon can not be / But contentacyon without pleasure we se / In thynges innumerable euery day" (ll. 1105-7).[11] Later it revolves around a problem in definition—"Is not absens of displeasure a pleasure" (l. 1239). Lover-loved initially wins this dispute when he compares his opponent to a post which feels neither pleasure nor pain. Neither-lover-nor-loved retires from the stage, vowing that he will prove that his life is more pleasurable and has less pain. Lover-loved, who scoffs at this threat, relishes his victory: ". . . what a face this fole hath set here / Tyll shame defaced his foly so clere / That shame hath shamfully in syght of you all / With shame dryuen hens to his shamefull fall" (ll. 1270-73).

But his victory is short-lived; Neither-lover-nor-loved returns. The stage direction offers an interesting insight into early Tudor dramatic action: "Here the vyse cometh in ronnynge sodenly aboute the place among the audiens with a hye copyn tank on his hed full of squybs fyred cryeng watere water, fyre, fyre, fyre, water, water, fyre, tyll the fyre in the squybs be spent" (p. 200). Such excitement would arouse any of those in the audience that might have been dozing. We should also note that the reference to Neither-lover-nor-loved as a vice is one of the earliest occurrences of this word in English dramatic literature.

When Neither-lover-nor-loved hints that the house of the lover's betrothed is on fire, Lover-loved, in a state of despair, rushes out. The vice then roars at the trick he has played; there is no fire, but the torment that Lover-loved undergoes is obvious. He returns and attempts to recover his composure, but the vice continues to taunt him. Lover-loved again resorts to argument by analogy, comparing their situations to those of a tree and a horse. Neither-lover-nor-loved—the tree—has neither pain nor pleasure, whereas he at times—like the horse—may have pain but also much pleasure. Lover-loved draws the comparison out at length:

> For as a tree hath lyfe without felyng
> Wherby it felyth pleasyng nor displeasyng
> And can not be but contented quyetly
> Euen the lyke case is yours now presently
> And as the hors feleth payne and not the tre
> Lykewyse I haue payne and no payne haue ye
> And as a hors aboue a tre felyth pleasure

So fele I pleasure aboue you in rate sure
And as the tre felyth nother and the hors both
Euyn so pleasure and payne betwene vs twayne goeth.
(ll. 1433-42)

He then asks Lover-not-beloved and Beloved-not-loving to judge their claims on the basis of this analogy.

But the play ends without solving either argument. All agree they can see no difference between the pains and pleasures of the others. Neither-lover-nor-loved comments upon the one dispute: "Yet in my iudgement by these cases hath she / As great and as many felyng paynes as he" (ll. 1476-77). Both Lover-loved and Neither-lover-nor-loved are content with their own estates, and the other two disputants also graciously accept the decision. Lover-not-beloved draws the concluding moral:

Syns such contentacyon may hardely acorde
In such kynde of loue as here hath ben ment
Let vs seke the loue of that louyng lorde
Who to suffer passyon for loue was content
Wherby his louers that loue for loue assent
Shall haue in fyne aboue contentacyon
The felyng pleasure of eternall saluacyon.
(1560-66)

This quotation is also an example of the rhyme royal, in which Heywood writes the last one hundred lines. Most of the play is in tetrameter couplets, the meter that Heywood established as the usual vehicle for the Tudor interlude. Heywood does not use rhyme royal in either The Pardoner and the Friar or Johan Johan, but Weather opens with ninety-seven lines of rhyme royal (the first speech of Jupiter) and uses this stanza whenever Jupiter speaks at length (ll. 161-74; 179-85; 1123-29). In Weather Heywood makes a conscious attempt to fit the verse to the speaker.[12] The rest of the play is in the normal couplets.

If we enter into the spirit of this animated debate, Love, it is great fun; furthermore, the play offers as a partial distraction a fabliau tale that divides the play nicely into two parts and affords a useful change of pace. This play is manifestly superior to Witty and Witless. By doubling the debate, by introducing for the first time in secular drama the vice of the morality plays, and by suggesting some stage action and humor, Heywood has made a major advance in dramatic craftsmanship.

The subject that Heywood offered also had a unique appeal

in Tudor England. The pleasures and problems of love were a constant topic in the preceding centuries and continued to be so in the succeeding ones. John Lyly's *Euphues* is one manifestation of this interest. The poetry of Wyatt and Surrey, as they reflect the Petrarchan concepts of the man-woman relationship, portrays the pain and anguish of the Lover-not-loved and the woman Beloved-not-loving. Heywood's *Play of Love* is, therefore, a part of a continuing tradition.

The Play of the Weather marks another step in dramatic maturity. That *Weather* followed the previously discussed plays is of course a tenuous assumption, but there can be little doubt that it is superior to both *Witty* and *Love* because Heywood in *Weather* introduces a variety of characters who vary the pace of the play. Professor Hillebrand praises *Weather* for demonstrating "both the author's dramatic sense and his feeling for character."[13] The outline of the play is simple, but the construction is masterful; the pace is rapid.

Mark Twain said that everyone talks about the weather, but nobody does anything about it. In Heywood's play Jupiter, who decides to do something, issues a proclamation that all his subjects should petition him for establishing a certain weather pattern.[14] He appoints, after some haranguing, Mayster Mery-reporte to issue the proclamation and to interview the petitioners. Jupiter then retires to his throne; and Mery-reporte, who is described as the vice, takes over the stage. Jupiter's final instruction to Mery-reporte deserves note:

> Here to receyve all sewters of eche degre;
> And suche as to the may seme moste metely,
> We wyll thow brynge them before our maieste;
> And for the rest, that be not so worthy,
> Make thou reporte to us effectually,
> So that we may heare eche maner sewte at large.
>
> (ll. 168-73)

That Heywood is conscious of social distinctions is evident in his handling of the petitioners. A gentleman, a merchant, a ranger, a water-miller, a wind-miller, a gentlewoman, a laundress, and a little boy approach Jupiter; but only the gentleman and merchant are granted an audience. Furthermore, the very order of their approach suggests the hierarchy of Heywood's society.

The humor of the play exists on several levels. First, Heywood emphasizes the pretentiousness and egocentricity of each of the

petitioners; second, there is the obvious absurdity of the various
contradictory petitions; third, there is the immediate banter
between Mery-reporte and each petitioner, and twice (the
wind-miller and the water-miller; the gentlewoman and the
laundress) Heywood brings two opposing petitioners on stage
at the same time. The continuing variation not only keeps the
play entertaining but also removes it from the realm of mere
verbal quibbling and intellectual juggling.

The first to come before Jupiter's throne is a Gentleman who
wishes pleasant weather—"drye and not mysty, the wynde calme
and styll" (l. 274)—for the hunt. His pompous nature is evident
in his prefatory remarks:

> Most myghty prynce, and god of every nacyon,
> Pleasyth your hyghnes to vouchsave the herynge
> Of me, whyche, accordynge to your proclamacyon,
> Doth make apparaunce, in way of besechynge
> Not sole for my-self, but generally
> For all come of noble and auncyent stock,
> Whych sorte above all doth most thankfully
> Dayly take payne for welth of the comen flocke,
> With dylygent study alway devysynge
> To kepe them in order and unyte,
> In peace to labour the encrees of theyr lyvynge,
> Wherby eche man may prosper in plente.
>
> (ll. 258-69)[15]

The historical or political point should be obvious in this speech.
The Gentleman claims that the granting of his weather will
benefit the commonwealth, for he sees himself as the most
important part of the nation. The Merchant expresses a similar
self-conceit: "Who sholde afore us marchauntes accompted be?
/ For were not we, the worlde shuld wyshe and want / In many
thynges, whych now shall lack rehersall" (ll. 359-61). But
Mery-reporte who respects no person, suggests that the Gentleman's horns manifest cuckoldry, not hunting skill; and he greets
the Merchant with a suggestive witticism: "Maysters person,
[parson] now welcome, by my lyfe! / I pray you, how doth my
masters, your wyfe?" (ll. 329-30).

The Merchant urges that the winds blow strongly to bring his
ships safely to port, but the winds must also be controlled. A
Ranger[16] then enters and desires storms—strong winds that will
topple trees which can then be sold for fuel. Three petitioners
want three different things—no wind; controlled wind; storms.

At this point, Heywood evidently realized that to continue the play in the same manner would be repetitious—for the absurdity of the proclamation is evident—and his dramatic sense turns to the actual conflict of character.

After a Water-miller pleads for rain—the wind blows so strongly that there is never any rain—the Wind-miller enters and cries: "The wynde is so weyke it sturryth not our stonys" (l. 511). The combatants are introduced; and, as Mery-reporte slips off stage, they argue the merits of their respective trades. Heywood obviously is satirizing the egocentricity of people who see themselves or their work as the be-all and end-all of the universe. The Wind-miller exposes his narrowness:

> But, in few wordes to tell you my mynde rounde;
> Uppon this concycyon I wolde be bounde
> Day by day to say Our Ladyes sauter
> That in this world were no drope of water,
> Nor never rayne, but wynde contynuall.
> Then shold we wynde myllers be lordes over all!
>
> (ll. 540-45)

The argument between the two millers turns on which can be best spared, water or wind. The Water-miller has a good case for himself since, as he points out, nothing could exist without water. Defeated in what we might call the "theoretical argument," the Wind-miller switches the subject to the more practical question—which mill is the more efficient? In this play Heywood does not introduce the dispassionate arbitrator, but the contemptuous judge; the argument is absurd; and Mery-reporte returns to silence them and, after some obscene jesting sends them off stage.

To counter the humor of these two millers, Heywood introduces two women—a Gentlewoman and a Laundress. Just as Mery-reporte had implied that the gentleman had been cuckolded, he now jests suggestively with the Gentlewoman. The exchange is coarse, but it is typical of much Tudor humor:

> Gentylwoman.
> I knew not how to passe in to the god now.
> Mery-reporte.
> No, but ye know how he may passe into you.
> Gentylwoman.
> I pray you let me in at the backe syde.

> Mery-reporte.
> Ye, shall I so and your foresyde so wyde?
> Nay, not yet! But syns ye love to be alone,
> We twayne wyll into a corner anone.
>   (ll. 768-73)

Next Mery-reporte approaches the dignified Jupiter with this proposal:

> My lorde, how nowe! Loke uppe lustely!
> Here is a derlynge come, by Saynt Antony!
> And yf yt be your pleasure to mary,
> Speke quyckly, for she may not tary.
> In fayth, I thynke ye may wynne her anone,
> For she wolde speke wyth your lordshyp alone.
>   Jupyter.
> Sonne, that is not the thynge at this tyme ment.
> If her sewt concerne no cause of our hyther resorte,
> Sende her out of place; but yf she be bent
> To that purpose, heare her and make us reporte.
>   (ll. 780-89)

In such exchanges Heywood is at his best. The bustling, bouncing, incorrigible Mery-reporte, the dignified Jupiter, and the conceited, pompous ("What sholde I do where so mych people is?") Gentlewoman offer some sparkling contrasts. Of the ten characters in the play, the Gentlewoman is the most engaging. A type to be sure, her speeches, however, suggest a vivid, if contemptible personality. She is a minor Wife of Bath: "I am a woman ryght fayre, as ye se; / In no creature more beauty then in me is" (ll. 819-20). And the audience is also a part of a Heywood play; for, after Jupiter rebuffs Mery-reporte, he, the vice, comments to the audience, "I count women lost, yf we love them not well, / For ye se god loveth them never a dele!" (ll. 790-91).

The play turns to music as Mery-reporte and the Gentlewoman sing a duet; but, unfortunately, the song is not given. The level of the humor varies in this play, but it is often coarse as the entrance of the Laundress again manifests. Mery-reporte begs the lady for a kiss:

> What! yes, hardely! Kys me ons and no more.
> I never desyred to kys you before.
>   *Here the Launder cometh in.*
>   Launder.
> Why! have ye always kyst her behynde? (ll. 866-68)

The battle between the two women is abortive; the Laundress, who argues vehemently and emotionally, accuses the Gentlewoman of idleness and loose living; and she beseeches Mery-reporte to work for a hot sun for drying clothes. The Gentlewoman, strangely silent, finally retreats from the fray with a brief entreaty to Mery-reporte to remember her petition. Although the Gentlewoman and Laundress represent idleness and industry, respectively, Heywood makes no value judgment; and Mery-reporte scorns both.

The last petitioner is a brilliant stroke. The problem that the play presents—the egocentricity of each petitioner and the danger to society of such uncontrolled self-interest—is simply and humorously summarized in a small boy ("the lest that can play") whose pleasure is catching birds and throwing snowballs. And his final request skillfully satirizes the naïveté of each petitioner:

> Yf god of his wether wyll gyve nonny,
> I pray you, wyll he sell ony?
> Or lend us a bushell of snow, or twayne,
> And poynt us a day to pay hym agayne?
> (ll. 1041-44)

When Mery-reporte summarizes the sundry petitions and places the problem before Jupiter, he emphasizes that only a very wise judge could solve such a problem:

> Not one of theyr sewtes agreeth wyth an other.
> I promyse you, here is a shrewed pece of warke!
> This gere wyll trye wether ye be a clarke.
> Yf ye trust to me, yt is a great foly;
> For yt passeth my braynes, by goddes body!
> (ll. 1118-22)

But Jupiter handles the problem tactfully; he orders no changes in the weather, but tells each petitioner that he will often have the exact weather he has requested. Jupiter makes this necessity sound like a special favor:

> Myche better have we now devysed for ye all
> Then ye all can perceyve, or coude desyre.
> Eche of you sewd to have contynuall
> Suche wether as his crafte onely doth requyre.
> All wethers in all places yf men all tymes myght hyer,
> Who could lyve by other? What is this neglygens
> Us to atempt in suche inconvenyens!
> (ll. 1183-89)

Jupiter then emphasizes the interdependence of one craft upon another and the necessity of cooperation between such sundry factions. Overwhelmed by Jupiter's wisdom, each petitioner pays tribute to such a benign ruler. In each speech the delineation of the character is continued, as the small boy's speech witnesses, "Godfather god, I wyll do somwhat for you agayne. / By Cryste, ye may happe to have a byrd or twayne! / And I promyse you, yf any snow come, / When I make my snow-ballys ye shall have some" (ll. 1235-38). The play ends with Jupiter, in two stanzas of rhyme royal, congratulating himself upon the peaceful settlement of the dispute.

The irony of the conclusion is manifold. The petitioners who had wanted a specific weather now claim they are satisfied. Jupiter, who had boasted that he would change the weather to everyone's best advantage, now realizes he can do nothing. The first two lines of his closing speech ring with ambiguity: "We nede no whyte our selfe any farther to bost, / For our dedes declare us apparauntly" (ll. 1241-42). Nothing is accomplished; nothing is changed; yet the problem is solved. The status quo is vindicated.

Just as *The Spider and the Fly* paid a graceful tribute to Queen Mary and advocated the necessity of a strong, benevolent ruler, *The Play of the Weather* develops a similar theme. There must be some final judge in disputes, for the ordinary individual sees the problem from a very limited perspective and himself as all-important. Just as Jupiter handles the egocentric petitioners, a strong ruler can pacify the feuding factions.

How far such general statements should be applied to the specific facts of Heywood's England is, of course, questionable. Perhaps some of Heywood's audience saw a direct connection between Jupiter, the ruler of earth, and Henry VIII, the ruler of England. There is nothing, however, in the play that suggests a personal allusion to the reigning monarch. Surely *Weather* is a compliment to the king, and its theme supports the concept of a wise and benevolent monarch; but it is fruitless to speculate about its political aspects.[17]

But the student of the developing Tudor drama is more interested in the dramatic importance of *Weather*. Heywood's play demonstrates the limits to which the debate mold can be stretched; he has now added characterization and a fast-moving pace that debate itself does not insure. By continually introducing new characters, Heywood insures sustained interest; but the continuity of the play depends upon the central idea. This play employs an absurd situation that wears well even after several readings, but it is difficult to suggest other topics that could be handled in such an artificial manner. Heywood demonstrates here a dramatic sense, and in the next plays we discuss Heywood discards the debate format and develops a more dramatic structure.

In these three plays the humanist dominates the dramatist. Although a cursory reading might emphasize the humor and although an audience drowsy after a full meal might only respond to the obvious, the plays are social commentaries. Heywood explores the true definition of wisdom, the various pleasures and pains of the lover, and the importance of a strong, wise ruler. These plays reflect at a popular level—for they are interludes to be performed after supper—[18] the thinking of the More circle. Heywood is a link between the originators of ideas and the educated society, and his early plays are products of the humanistic fervor of the early part of the century. "Consciously or unconsciously, he approached the serious ideas of More, Erasmus, Rastell, and Vives, when he stressed the contributions which common men like the Wind Miller make to the commonweal and the difficulties a ruler meets when he tries to give justice to all."[19]

We should not assume that Heywood necessarily abandoned the debate form as undramatic and turned to farce. Dating the plays and establishing some sort of order must be handled in detail later, but we must mention here another Heywood play that has only recently been discovered. Its discovery should destroy any argument for dating that depends exclusively on the theory that the less dramatic debates preceded the farces.

A fragment of at least one other play—"Of the Parts of Man" —has been preserved in the autobiography of Thomas Whythorne, who served as Heywood's secretary from 1545 to 1548 and who thought very highly of his master, comparing him to Chaucer. The first assumption that we can make from this play is that Heywood was a much more active dramatist than his extant canon suggests. But more interesting is the fact that this play is obviously a debate that was written sometime between 1545 and 1548, many years after Heywood had written *Weather*, *Love*, and, we assume, the unpublished *Witty*.

The play is first mentioned by Thomas Whythorne thus:

"wh)y⟨ll I w⟩az with h⟨im, he mad dive)r⟨z⟩ ditt⟨iez to⟩ bee
sung vnto muzi⟨kall⟩ instrumen⟨ts⟩ (also hee ⟨caw⟩zed ⟨to⟩ be
prin⟨ted A⟩ book mad vpon owr ⟨en⟩glysh proverbz) And also
at þe request of doktor ⟨Thos.⟩ Cranmer, lat a⟨rchb⟩yshop of
Cantorbury, hee mad A sertayn enter⟨lude⟩ or play, þe which
waz devyzed vpon þe parts of Man, at þe end wherof hee
lykneth and applieth þe sirkumstans þerof to þe vniuersall
estat of Chrýstes church."[20] Later in his autobiography, when
he is discussing reason, Whythorne quotes fourteen lines from
the play. Although he claims that the play is in verse, Whythorne
renders the passage in prose. Reason has claimed superiority
and government over man and over all living things:

And þe diffrens between man þe kommaunder, and beas⟨ts⟩ being
by man kommaunded, iz only Reazon in man, þe disserner of good and
ill, þe good in man elekted by me, and þ'ill in man by mee reʒected,
man obeing mee shýnth in exsellensy, and disobeing mee, shewth
mans insolensy. Now sin⟨s I⟩ reazon am þ' ⟨o⟩nly qu⟨a⟩lyte, þa⟨t
q⟩ualifiet man ⟨in s⟩uch A temp⟨er⟩ans az setteth man in plạs of
prinsipalite abọv all beasts to stand in gove⌈r⌉nans who but I over
man shiuld him self advans, to govern lýkwyz, sins I bring man
þerto, and keep man þerin doing az I bid him do.[21]

The quotation above is most likely from the beginning of the
play, for Whythorne then adds that Will enters to dispute with
Reason over which of them should rule over man: "Whervpon
in þe end þei both ar dryven to graunt þat man kan do nothing
withowt will, and withowt reazon man kan do no good thing."[22]
The debate thus ends in a draw.

It is difficult to comment upon the play on the basis of fourteen lines and the comments of Heywood's secretary. The play
that "The Parts of Man" seems most similar to is *Witty and
Witless*, which is almost universally considered to be Heywood's
first dramatic effort. "The Parts of Man" may have only two
characters, Will and Reason who dispute· over the problem of
supremacy. In the pages immediately preceding the quotation
from Heywood's play, Whythorne discusses the difference between wit and wisdom. In *Witty and Witless* Jerome had
claimed that one can be witty without being wise; and Whythorne echoes this idea and claims that the witty one might
be evil unless he is ruled by reason. He offers a "sonnet" he
composed on the subject:

When witt doth seek výs to embrạs
þen witt him self doth much defạs

> for witt and wizdom diffreth so
> az witt from wizdom needs must go
> if witt by wizdom rewll in plạs
> (as reazon wold it shiuld be so)
> þen witt so wurking yee shall see
> will wurk all well in ech degree,
> but if witt wurk withowt wizdom
> I dowt what good þerof will kom.[23]

One conclusion must be suggested. If *Witty* is Heywood's first play, "The Parts of Man" written some thirty years later may cover a closely related subject and may be a debate with little if any characterization or dramatic conflict. Obviously Heywood never discarded the debate genre as some scholars have suggested.[24]

III *The Farces*

When we turn to the farces, however, we can more easily recognize a dramatic sense. These plays—*Pardoner and Friar, Four PP,* and *Johan Johan*—established Heywood's reputation as the outstanding dramatist of early Tudor England. Because *The Four PP* is still in many ways a debate, it is a convenient transition between the debates (already discussed) and the two pure farces.

The Four PP revolves around a contest for supremacy between a Palmer, a Pardoner, and a Pothecary. The fourth *P* is a Pedler who is the judge of the dispute. The central episode—a lying contest (the two tales themselves are entertaining, if coarse)— is brilliantly handled; but the play is padded with a moralistic, anticlimactic argument and with an occasionally tedious opening exchange. Heywood has still not developed the concentration upon the specific incident that is essential to dramatic conflict.

The interlude opens with the Palmer,[25] who recounts his extensive travels and glorifies his journeys as the best road to salvation:

> For, be ye sure, I thynke surely
> Who seketh sayntes for Crystes sake—
> And namely such as payne do take
> On fote to punyshe their frayle body—
> Shall thereby meryte more hyely
> Then by any thinge done by man.
>
> (ll. 58-63)

The Pardoner enters to scoff at the Palmer's naïveté and to satirize his motives. The Pardoner offers instant salvation: Why travel to Rome when he is at the doorstep with his pardons? The easiest way to salvation is, therefore, through him. But the Pothecary now enters to insist all must wait upon him: "No soule, ye knowe, entreth heuen gate / Tyll from the bodye he be separate; / And whome haue ye knowen dye ho[ne]stlye / Without helpe of the potycary?" (ll. 169-72).

The disputants now need a judge and a more specific subject. The first necessity is furnished by the Pedler who enters with his pack. And we should note here that this play has an obvious visual appeal: the Pardoner has with him a packet of pardons and relics, and the Pothecary also carries his packet of medicines; in the course of the play, they pull objects from their bags to exemplify their vocations. Since the Pedler is the only one of the four who is not involved with death, his introduction is a digression or interlude of sorts; but in the total structure of the play, it is a preliminary attack upon women. The play pokes fun at the two religious types portrayed on the stage, but it also satirizes women, a constant topic of Heywood's poetry. The Pothecary innocently questions what he carries in his pack, and for the next sixty-five lines the Pedler boasts of his marvelous merchandise and offers witticisms about the pretensions of clerics and women.

The introductions over, Heywood has his four actors exchange some verbal quibbling about the cause and effect of drinking and sleeping; and they finally lapse into a song which is not given. All of this quibbling may be satisfactory entertainment after a heavy dinner, but it is not drama. Not only could many of the speeches be eliminated, but there is neither any advance in the plot nor development of a specific conflict. It is instead a scene of four men insulting and badgering one another with no definite reason or goal. The Pardoner, however, remembers the original disagreement and in a long speech recalls the point at issue before the Pedler had entered. Dramatically, this speech is the most crass form of exposition; but, given the conditions of the performance of the play—as an interlude after a meal in some lord's home—it may have been necessary.

We should recall that *Love* also has what might be labled a false start, the double debate occurring after the *fabliau* tale offered by Neither-lover-nor-loved. And Mery-reporte offers a long summary of the petitioners in Heywood's *Play of the Weather* (11. 1069-1122). Perhaps Heywood included such speeches to guide his audience through the evening's entertainment. In *The Four PP* the first part of the play sets the mood and engages the audience; then, when the audience is more receptive, the plot is restated and the play can start once again. At least, after the Pardoner's speech the exchange is more rapid and spirited, although it is still a repetition of previously handled ideas:

> PEDLER: Why, do potycaries kyll men?
> POTYCARY: By God, men say so now and then!
> PEDLER: And I thought ye wolde nat have myst
> To make men lyue as longe as ye lyste.
> POTYCARY: As longe as we lyste? nay, longe as they can!
> PEDLER: So myght we lyue without you than.
> POTYCARY: Ye, but yet it is necessary
> For to haue a potycary;
> For when ye fele your conscyens redy,
> I can sende you to heuen quyckly.
>
> (ll. 366-75)

The Pedler is asked to judge which of the three is the most important, but Heywood is didactic even when entertaining; through the Pedler, he manifests a faith in the office, if a contempt for the individual officeholder. The contest can not be conducted on an abstract level; a pedler can only judge a more specific debate:

> I neyther wyll iudge the beste nor worste;
> For, be ye bleste or be ye curste,
> Ye know it is no whyt my sleyght
> To be a iudge in maters of weyght.
> It behoueth no pedlers nor proctours
> To take on them iudgemente as doctours.
> But yf your myndes be onely set
> To worke for soule helthe, ye be well met,
> For eche of you somwhat doth showe
> That soules towarde heuen by you do growe.
>
> (ll. 382-91)

But each of the knaves still demands priority. The Pedler finally suggests that he could surely judge a lying contest—a fair trial, indeed, since all three are so proficient in this skill.

The play now has a focal conflict, but Heywood still digresses; instead of moving to the contest, Heywood allows the Pardoner and the Pothecary to display the treasures of their packs. The digression is prompted by the Palmer's innocent remark, when he acquiesces with the decision to determine the order of mastery through a lying contest—"And sure I thynke that quietnesse / In any man is great rychesse" (ll. 478-79). The Pardoner, who scoffs at such sentiment, asks if such riches will buy food when one is hungry. Instead, the Pardoner sees his claim of authority bolstered by his holdings; his relics are sources of power. He prefaces his display thus:

> Nay, yf rychesse myghte rule the roste,
> Behold what cause I haue to boste!
> [*He opens his pack.*]
> Lo, here be pardons halfe a dosyn.
> For gostely ryches they haue no cosyn.
> (ll. 486-89)

The Pothecary replies similarly:

> If I haue neuer the more for the,
> Then be the relykes no ryches to me,
> Nor to thy-selfe, excepte they be
> More benefycyall then I can se.
> [*He opens his pocket of medicines.*]
> Rycher is one boxe of [t]his tryacle
> Then all thy relykes that do no myrakell.
> (ll. 580-85)

Although there are humorous exchanges as each viewer scoffs at the displays, it is a false start in the actual contest.

Finally the Pothecary begins his lie (l. 708). He tells a *fabliau* story of a marvelous cure he had performed upon a young woman who suffered from the falling sickness. To stop her system, he had placed "a tampyon in her tewell." The results were disastrous for a neighboring castle, but salutary for the young woman. "But when this tampyon on this castel lyght, / It put the castels so farre to flyght / That downe they came eche vpon other, / No stone lefte standynge, by Goddes Mother!" (ll. 750-53).

The Pardoner's lie also concerns a woman, one whom he had rescued from Hell[26]—a short tale that is a masterpiece of imaginative detail and selected satire. The Pardoner had journeyed to the underworld in an attempt to retrieve this friend who had died so suddenly that she had not repented of her sins. Not finding her in Purgatory, the Pardoner journeys on to Hell; "for with her lyfe I was so acqueynted / That sure I

thought she was nat saynted" (ll. 811-12). When he sneezes, a
soul calls "Christe helpe." The Pardoner uses all his powers and
pardons to send him straight to Heaven. The devil at the gate
of Hell is an old friend who "oft in the play of Corpus Cristi
/ . . . hath played the deuyll at Couentry" (ll. 831-32). The
devils are celebrating the anniversary of Lucifer's fall, so every
reasonable request will be granted (Heywood digresses for a
few lines to describe the dress of the devils). The Pardoner,
granted a safe-conduct pass, presents his plea personally to
Lucifer who, upon hearing which devil he requests, is happy
to release her:

> "Now, by our honour" sayd Lucyfer,
> "No deuyll in hell shall witholde her!
> And yf thou woldest haue twenty mo,
> Were nat for iustyce, they shulde goo.
> For all we deuyls within thys den
> Haue more to do with two women
> Then with all the charge we haue besyde.
> Wherfore, yf thou our frende wyll be tryed,
> Aply thy pardons to women so
> That vnto vs there come no mo."
>
> (ll. 933-42)

Heywood's climax is brilliant. He has presented two tales that
center around women, the last one being a direct attack upon
all women. The Palmer now comments upon the Pardoner's
tale, expressing surprise that women in Hell are so shrewish:

> Yet in all places where I haue ben,
> Of all the women that I haue sene,
> I never sawe, nor knewe, in my consyens,
> Any one woman out of paciens.
>
> (ll. 1001-4)

The reaction is instantaneous:

> POTYCARY: By the masse, there is a great lye!
> PARDONER: I neuer harde a greater, by Our Lady!
> PEDLER: A greater? nay, knowe ye any so great?
>
> (ll. 1005-7)

The contest is over; the opponents have reacted honestly, if
without thinking. When the Pedler awards victory to the Palmer,
the play should end; the climax would be artistically perfect,
but the humanist overpowers the dramatist, and the play plods

along for some two hundred more lines as the Pardoner and
Pothecary refuse to accept the obvious judgment that they
themselves announced. Realizing that his position of leadership
would be tenuous at best, the Palmer releases the Pardoner and
Pothecary from their bond of obedience. But the play is still not
over, for the Pedler addresses himself to the two clerics and
delivers a fifty-line sermon. The ideals of both the Palmer and
the Pardoner must be admired; the problem is not the idea but
the practice, as the two performers in *The Four PP* have demonstrated. The Pedler stresses a serious religious point in this
speech:

> For, though ye walke nat both one waye,
> Yet, walkynge thus, thys dare I saye:
> That bothe your walkes come to one ende.
> And so for all that do pretende,
> By ayde of Goddes grace, to ensewe
> Any maner kynde of vertue:
> As, some great almyse for to gyue,
> Some in wyllfull pouertie to lyue,
> Some to make hye-wayes and suche other warkes,
> And some to mayntayne prestes and clarkes
> To synge and praye for soule departed,—
> These, with all other vertues well marked,
> All-though they be of sondry kyndes;
> Yet be they nat vsed with sondry myndes;
> But, as God only doth all those moue,
> So euery man, onely for His loue,
> With loue and dred obediently
> Worketh in these vertues vnyformely.
>
> (ll. 1155-72)

The Palmer and Pardoner thus follow a virtuous and admirable
path; one obvious fault is that each scoffs at the virtue of the
other. In this play we see Heywood praising the church itself
while at the same time satirizing the corrupt individuals within
the framework; moreover, such criticism is absolutely necessary
as the subsequent exchange with the Pothecary demonstrates. The
Pothecary asks the penetrating question of how can one revere
those relics which are obviously false. The Pedler—here we must
substitute Heywood, for the Pedler is out of character once the
lying contest is over—again contrasts the ideal with the practice.
One can criticize, but there are limitations which are delineated
by the church, the final authority. In the 1520's the Pedler's

speech is especially appropriate; for it is a partial analysis of the questioning, skeptical age which was still inchoate and of which Heywood was a part:

> For his, and all other that ye knowe fayned,
> Ye be nother counceled nor constrayned
> To any suche thynge in any suche case
> To gyue any reuerence in any suche place;
> But where ye dout the truthe, nat knowynge,
> Beleuynge the beste, good may be growynge.
> In iudgynge the beste, no harm at the leste,
> In iudgynge the worste, no good at the beste.
> But beste in these thynges, it semeth to me,
> To take no iudgement vpon ye;
> But, as the Churche doth iudge or take them,
> So do ye receyue or forsake them;
> And so, be sure, ye can nat erre,
> But may be a frutfull folower.
>
> (ll. 1205-18)

The Palmer then closes the play with two stanzas of rhyme royal asking for God's grace and apologizing for any offensive passages. The dispute then was ephemeral, for the four men are reunited under God's love; the dispute is dramatic; the theme, didactic.

It is easy to mistake the means for the end in this play, for the reader can be misled by the satirical attacks upon women. After the lies have been told, the Pedler supports his decision by relating his own ideas. He claims that one will find two out of every three women to be shrews and may often find all three shrewish. That women are never out of patience is a monstrous lie. The play reaches a peak of boisterous satire here as the Pedler defends his decision and the Pothecary and the Pardoner refuse to accept his judgment. According to the rules of the contest, the Pothecary and the Pardoner now must attend on the Palmer; but they refuse, and the Palmer wisely releases them from their obligation.

Now Heywood attempts to switch from the comic, the satirical to the serious, the moral. Satire against women is only a part of the drama; the theme of the play is not woman's foibles but the serious problem of church reform. The opening problem in the play is the question of mastery: Who is the best of the three? Initially, they argue about their efficacy in sending souls to heaven, but since the Pedler can not judge them on this basis, they decide on a lying contest to prove their order of importance. Obviously entertainment is all-important here, but entertainment is not the main concern for a Christian humanist like Heywood. The spiritual question of mastery can not be solved by the Palmer's brilliant witticism, even if the dramatic question can be.

Thus the Pedler becomes serious and advocates in a lengthy speech the concept that the Pardoner and the Palmer, though they follow different paths, seek the same goals and are equal in God's sight. To despise another type of virtue is wrong, for the two types of virtue—that of the ideal Palmer and the ideal Pardoner—are equal. When the Pothecary counters that he is thankful he uses no virtue at all, the Palmer again praises the virtuous life and cautions him about condemning those things of which he has not sufficient knowledge; instead one must follow the judgments of the church. In these last hundred lines the amateur polemicist controls the incipient dramatist.

Despite its many faults, *The Four PP* is Heywood's most engaging play. The four characters develop distinct personalities, and the Pedler is an entertaining master of ceremonies. The Pardoner's tale is a brilliantly appropriate, well-unified story, and the climax of the play could not be improved upon. The play could be successfully performed today.

If these four plays can firmly be assigned to Heywood on the basis of both internal and external evidence, we may move to *The Pardoner and the Friar* without the benefit of external proof. Internally, the spirit of this play is the same as that of the other plays. The Pardoners of *The Four PP* and *The Pardoner and the Friar* are direct descendants of Chaucer's Pardoner, as Heywood has in *The Pardoner and the Friar* appropriated Chaucer's language as well as his relics.[27] Heywood has borrowed a lengthy passage from "The Pardoner's Prologue";

> Thanne have I in latoun a sholder-boon
> Which that was of an hooly Jewes sheep.
> "Goode men," I seye, "taak of my wordes keep;
> If that this boon be wasshe in any welle,
> If cow, or calf, or sheep, or oxe swelle
> That any worm hath ete, or worm ystonge,
> Taak water of that welle and wassh his tonge,
> And it is hool anon; and forthermoore,
> Of pokkes and of scabbe, and every soore
> Shal every sheep be hool that of this welle
> Drynketh a draughte. Taak kep eek what I telle:

> If that the good-man that the beestes oweth
> Wol every wyke, er that the cok hym croweth,
> Fastynge, drynken of this welle a draughte,
> As thilke hooly Jew oure eldres taughte,
> His beestes and his stoor shal multiplie.
>
> And, sires, also it heeleth jalousie;
> For though a man be falle in jalous rage,
> Lat maken with this water his potage,
> And nevere shal he moore his wyf mystriste,
> Though he the soothe of hir defaute wiste,
> Al had she taken prestes two or thre.
>
> Heere is a miteyn eek, that ye may se.
> He that his hand wol putte in this mitayn
> He shal have multipliyng of his grayn,
> Whan he hath sowen, be it whete or otes,
> So that he offre pens, or elles grotes.
>
> Goode men and wommen, o thyng warne I yow:
> If any wight be in this chirche now
> That hath doon synne horrible, that he
> Dar nat, for shame, of it yshryven be,
> Or any womman, be she yong or old,
> That hath ymaad hir housbonde cokewold,
> Swich folk shal have no power ne no grace
> To offren to my relikes in this place.
> And whoso fyndeth hym out of swich blame,
> He wol come up and offre in Goddes name,
> And I assoille him by the auctoritee
> Which that by bulle ygraunted was to me."
>   (VI[C] 350-88)

The Pardoner here mentions two relics, both of which Heywood uses in his play almost verbatim. Heywood's handling of the magical powers of the holy bone should serve as a sufficient comparison, for both cure jealousy equally well. Although Chaucer refers to it as a shoulder bone of a holy Jew's sheep, for Heywood it is a bone from a holy Jew's hip. Heywood obviously had his copy of Chaucer before him as he wrote:

> And maysters all it helpeth well
> Thoughe a man be foule in ielous rage
> Let a man with this water make his potage
> And neuermore shall he his wyfe mystryst
> Thoughe he in sothe the faut by her wyst
> Or had she be take with freres two or thre.
>   (*Pardoner and Friar*, 150-51)

Then Heywood describes the efficacy of the mitten. After this, however, Heywood offers several other relics that are not found in Chaucer; the blessed arm of Saint Sunday, the great toe of the Trinity, the bongrace of the Virgin Mary, the blessed jawbone of All-Hallows, and the "brain pan" of Saint Michael which cures headaches. Heywood again returns to Chaucer for the closing exhortation to the audience.

Of the relics that Heywood did not borrow from Chaucer, two appear in *The Four PP*. There the Pardoner mentions briefly "Of All-Hallows the blessyd iaw-bone,— / Kys it hardely, with good deuocion" (ll. 497-98); but he does not describe its value as his counterpart in *The Pardoner and the Friar* does; this relic is an antidote against poison. The second relic that is mentioned twice is the toe of the Trinity, which Heywood borrows not from Chaucer but from himself:

> Nay, syrs, beholde, here may ye se
> The great-toe of the Trinite.
> Who to thys toe any money voweth,
> And ones may role it in his moueth,
> All hys lyfe after, I vndertake,
> He shall be ryd of the toth-ake.
> (Four PP, ll. 508-13)

> And another holy relyke here may ye see
> The great too of the holy trynyte
> And who so euer ones dothe it in his mouthe take
> He shall neuer be dysseasyd with the tothe ake
> Canker nor pockys shall there none brede
> This that I shewe ye is matter in dede.
> (Pardoner and Friar, 151)

The question, of course, arises as to which play came first— a question that allows no easy answer. The two plays may have a common source, a problem that I will discuss in detail in the following chapter; but some of the more obvious problems can be broached here. To argue that, since *The Pardoner and the Friar* depends heavily on Chaucer, it precedes (or follows) *The Four PP*, is obviously a tenuous argument. Perhaps even the assumption that they both were written during the same period is questionable.

Both Harold Newcomb Hillebrand and A. W. Reed claim that *The Pardoner and the Friar* is an earlier work than *The Four PP*. Reed dates *The Pardoner and the Friar* around 1519 and

The Four PP, 1520-21. Hillebrand says 1521 and 1525, respectively. J. E. Bernard insists that *The Pardoner and the Friar* is Heywood's earliest work. Bolwell, on the other hand, is more reluctant to suggest dates, but implies that *The Pardoner and the Friar* is a later play than usually suggested.[28]

One line in *The Pardoner and the Friar,* often used to date the play,[29] is the Pardoner's "Worshypfull maysters ye shall understand / That Pope Leo the X hath graunted with his hand" (153). Since Leo X died in 1521, the play may have been written before his death; but the satire would not be less effective after his death. Moreover, the Pardoner mentions several other Popes—Boniface IX (1389-1404), Julius (no number is given); Julius VI (a fictitious Pope or a misprint since only three Popes took the name Julius, Julius II ruling from 1503-13); and Innocent (again no number is given, but Innocent VIII reigned from 1484-92). By 1527, Henry VIII and Clement VII were disputing the validity of Henry's marriage to Catharine of Aragon. If the play was written this late, tact might have prevented Heywood from mentioning the reigning Pope. In fact, I doubt if a loyal Catholic like Heywood would have associated his knavish Pardoner with a living Pope.

A. W. Pollard has offered another argument for a late dating of the plays. He points to line 635 in *Weather*: "How rayne hath pryced corne within this vii yere." "The reference here is, I think, clearly to the great rains of the autumn of 1527 and April and May, 1528. . . ."[30] The line is surely too vague to support such a definite dating, but there is nothing in the play that would not allow *Weather* to be placed in the last few years of the decade.

Another interesting possibility which should be mentioned is a letter, found by Sidney Thomas, written by the French ambassador on January 1, 1529, which may have some bearing on Heywood's activities at court: "I think Wolsey would not be well pleased if I did not tell you of his causing farces to be played in French, with great display, saying in conclusion, that he does not wish anything to be here which is not French in deed and in word."[31] Such a demand may have directed Heywood's attention to French farce, the result of which was *The Pardoner and the Friar* and *Johan Johan.*

Critics agree that the six extant plays should be placed within Heywood's initial period of court activity, approximately 1519-

28. The printing date offers a positive *terminus ad quem,* but the spirit of the times must also be considered. In 1533 the Catholic Church was under serious attack from both Henry and from Luther. Heywood's plays that held corrupt clerics up for satirical attack would have found a ready audience in 1533; but his satire—critical and not destructive—would reform the institution, not destroy it. His plays reflect a less tumultuous time, a period when internal reform was a realistic possibility envisioned by such men as Erasmus and More. All of the six plays would be delightfully appropriate in the 1520's, and I suggest 1528 as a fairly late date for their composition. *Witty* probably was an early effort, written sometime after Heywood's appearance at court in 1519.

It would be convenient if Wesley Phy's ordering of the plays was beyond dispute. He lists the six plays in the "order of their dramatic development"; each play marks an advance "in dramatic unity, in the handling of stage effects, in the portraiture of characters, in the fluency and interest of the lines, and in sophistication of taste."[32] The order is *Witty, Love, Weather, Four PP, The Pardoner and the Friar,* and *Johan Johan.* That this development allows no room for "The Parts of Man" should demonstrate that it is difficult to impose later dramatic and artistic standards upon Heywood's so-called development. Although the reader may find it difficult to believe that Heywood wrote *Love* after *Weather* or *The Four PP,* we should not insist upon any strict chronology. To place the six extant plays within a ten- or twelve-year period and to suggest that they divide into two groups—debates and farces—is as far as we can safely go.

Still we can compare *The Pardoner and the Friar* and *The Four PP* as companion pieces even though we cannot argue for a specific order. *The Pardoner and the Friar* does have a unity and simplicity that *The Four PP* only suggests. Furthermore, *The Pardoner and the Friar* manifests for the first time the essential characteristics of farce. In one sense the play is more successful than *The Four PP,* for it concentrates upon a single incident, allowing no digression. Again we have the debate for mastery, this time between a pardoner and a friar; but there is no judge except the audience. And this play is designed for the stage, for the give-and-take of two vociferous, spirited actors who rudely interrupt and shout above one another.

More important, we can no longer argue that *The Pardoner*

and the Friar is didactic. A message may be implied, but it is not belabored. Even more surprising, the two rogues triumph in the end; they beat up the curate and Neighbor Pratt, who attempt to drive them from the church, and stroll off arm in arm, perhaps to the nearest tavern. The genre is hardly recognizable; the debate is wholly transformed into a contest for mastery. The combatants fight to a draw and then turn upon new opponents. Hypocrisy and deception seem to pay. Yet the Parson had welcomed both the Pardoner and the Friar to his church, and surely pardoners and friars should contribute much to the local parish. But Heywood is again contrasting the ideal and the actual. The underlying assumption is that the fault is in the individual, not in the church universal.

The play opens with this hypocritical Friar describing the ideal to which all friars should adhere: concern for the salvation of others; disregard for bodily wants, such as clothing and food. Finishing his introductory speech, the Friar kneels to pray; the Pardoner enters and begins to display his relics to the assembled congregation. In this play, as in the other Heywood interludes, the audience is an integral part of the dramatic performance. The dinner guests become members of the congregation, and the reader must imagine the intimacy between actor and audience which is a requisite of Tudor drama.

The Pardoner and the Friar is a short, fast-moving play. Once the two introductory speeches are over, the two shout out their lines in tetrameter couplets. Each speaks in couplets, but the rhyme scheme while both are speaking is *abab*. The play is difficult to read, but I assume that it would be easier to follow on stage, although the delivery of such lines would tax the skill of the actors to avoid a mere jumble. Whether they alternated the lines or spoke together I can not say, but the speeches are carefully developed, and surely Heywood wanted the audience to follow each argument. A short selection demonstrates the method:

> F: Maysters I shewed you ere whyle of almes dede
> P: Maysters this pardon whiche I shewed you before
> F: And how ye shulde gyue poore folke at theyr nede
> P: Is the greatest that euer was syth god was bore
> F: And yf of your partes that thynge ones were don
> P: For why without confessyon or contrycyon
> F: Dout not but god sholde gyue retrybucyon
> P: By this shall ye have clene remyssyon

> F: But now further it ought to be declared
> P: And forgyuen of the synnes seuen
> F: Who be thes pore folke that shold haue your reward.
>
> (160-61)

The play alternates between these dual solicitations of the audience and vitriolic attacks between the two clerics, until the two attempt to settle the dispute by fighting. At that point, the Parson and Neighbor Pratt attempt to drive them from the church; but the two scoundrels are triumphant and leave the Parson and Pratt bloody and beaten.

In the five plays so far discussed, we have noted some sort of progression from pure debate to incipient drama; and in *The Pardoner and the Friar* the contest for mastery results in dramatic conflicts—both verbal and finally physical. The dialogue is extremely well handled, an obvious improvement over the stilted speeches of *Witty*. Perhaps more important, the verbal quibbling that characterized all four of the other plays is absent; and there is a concentration inherent in this play that the other plays always lacked. I can not go so far, however, as to praise the plot, for here also Heywood has not constructed a firm plot; only in *Johan Johan* is a controlling plot present, and it is not of Heywood's construction.

Another virtue of *The Pardoner and the Friar* is that the conclusion has no edifying moral. That the Pardoner and Friar finally resort to physical abuse is appropriate for these two, and that the scoundrels unite to defeat the forces of good may not be edifying but is at least dramatically appropriate. In this play debate has degenerated into farce; but, for the perceptive, contemporary audience, there were also two burlesqued sermons.[33] The play also manifests a maturity of control and concentration that should preclude dismissing it as an early work. Effective drama does not permit digression, and in *The Pardoner and the Friar* Heywood does not digress.

Johan Johan should perhaps be assigned to Heywood only tentatively. Externally, evidence is lacking; but internally, the style is similar. In this play Heywood completely discards the debate genre and offers a tightly constructed plot; but we are discussing a translation, not an original effort. Most praise for plot and characterization must go to an anonymous French writer, but Heywood does make significant changes, which are discussed in the next chapter. The spirit of the play, at least, was not foreign to Heywood; for satire is again directed at the clergy, as it has been in the two other farces. But this time the satire is more integral, and it is more the individual priest than the type that is the target. Skillful characterization of all three roles—the naïve, dominated husband; the shrewish, dominating wife; the sly, profligate priest—is the salient feature of this work. The play has a dramatic unity comparable to, but superior to, *The Pardoner and the Friar.*

Johan Johan, the husband, opens this short interlude (only 678 lines) with a long monologue with the audience in which he berates his wife and vows that he will assert his masculine superiority. But Johan Johan is plagued with doubts; he realizes, as does the audience, that all this talk is mere bravado. His wife's entrance while he is boasting creates the humor of confusion with which the play abounds.

Actually, there is in this play, even more so than in Heywood's other plays, another participant—the audience. In his opening monologue Johan Johan is not so much performing before an audience as with the spectators. His opening lines suggest this byplay—"God spede you maysters, everychone! / Wote ye not whyther my wyfe is gone?" And both Tyb, the wife, and Johan Johan intersperse their argument with asides. At one level Johan Johan is the meek, submissive husband, and at the other level he confides to the audience his true thoughts.

The audience participation reaches its climax around line 242[34] when Johan Johan, commanded to move a table, seeks someone in the audience to hold his gown. He first offers it to one spectator but snatches it back with the cry, "But yet he shall not have it, by my fay; / He is so nere the dore he myght ron away" (ll. 252-53). Finally, he spies one in the audience he can trust: "But bycause that ye be trusty and sure, / Ye shall kepe it, and it be your pleasure; / And bycause it is arrayde at the skyrt, / Whyle ye do nothyng, skrape of the dyrt" (ll. 254-57). It is this intimate exchange between audience and actor that makes the Tudor interlude so unique and so difficult to appreciate in the study.

In the modern theater we sit and observe as if through the wall of a room; the soliloquies and asides which seemed so natural to the Elizabethan audience now strike us as strained and out of place. The only exchange between the performer and observer that suggests the intimacy of the interlude is the nightclub performer who often not only invites audience participation but often must handle unwanted participation. We must recall the anecdote that Roper relates of Sir Thomas More, who would occasionally enter a play with no rehearsal and improvise a part. The observer becomes participator. The roles are not always interchangeable, but the audience is an integral part of the play, not mere observer. Any attempt in the library to appreciate *Johan Johan* must admit this obvious inadequacy.

Johan Johan is ordered to invite Sir Johan, the village priest, to share a pie that Tyb, Sir Johan, and their friends had made that day. But each time he reaches the door, Tyb calls him back for one more domestic chore—wash the cups, move the stool. Johan Johan, meekly performing each chore, mumbles to the audience but avoids any confrontation with his wife.

The scene then shifts to the priest's house, where Sir Johan allays the cuckolded husband's suspicions first by refusing to come to supper and then by revealing that Tyb is angry with her confessor because he continually rebukes her. And she is a faithful wife—Johan Johan could not find a more loyal wife, for the priest has tested her:

> Yet thou thynkyst amys, peradventure,
> That of her body she shuld not be a good woman,
> But I shall tell the what I have done, Johan,
> For that matter; she and I be somtyme aloft,
> And I do lye uppon her many a time and oft
> To prove her; yet could I never espy
> That ever any dyd worse with her than I.
>
> (ll. 346-52)

Our sympathies move from Johan Johan; the braggart of the opening monologue becomes first the henpecked husband, then the naïve fool. He confides to the audience,

> I thought surely, so God me save,
> That he had lovyd my wyfe for to deseyve me.
> And now he quytyth hym-self; and here I se
> He doth as much as he may, for his lyfe,
> To stynte the debate betwene me and my wyfe.
>
> (ll. 370-74)

Johan Johan now urges his new friend to join them for dinner, especially since Sir Johan slyly reveals that he had planned to join several friends to eat a pie for which he had paid. Johan

Johan now insists that Sir Johan join them since the pie is at his house, but his dullness prevents him from asking where the other friends are—a problem that the priest, of course, avoids.

Back at the house, Johan is immediately sent to fetch water while Tyb and Sir Johan dally amorously. And, as he has all through the play, Johan Johan confides to the audience. He returns (without water for there is a hole in the bucket) and cries, "Cokkis soule, what have we here! / As far as I saw, he drewe very nere / Unto my wyfe" (ll. 439-41). Now Johan Johan is forced to mend the bucket and he kneels by the fire kneading the wax to patch the hole, alternately addressing his tormentors who are both flirting and enjoying the pie and muttering to the audience, his continual confidant.

When Tyb requests a tale of mirth for their after-dinner entertainment, Sir Johan responds with three miracles which he has witnessed. He first tells of a woman who had seven children in seven years although her husband was absent all that time; "Yet had she not had so many by thre / Yf she had not had the help of me" (ll. 547-48). Then he boasts of a woman barren of child for many years who, after a pilgrimage was, "delyvered of a chylde as moche as I. / How say you, is not this myracle wonderous?" (ll. 566-67). And finally he relates the story of another woman who was delivered of a full-grown child five months after her marriage. Such anti-clerical, anti-feminine sentiments remind the reader of the satire of *The Four PP*.

Johan Johan has had enough. Angry at missing the dinner, he berates his wife who feigns ignorance. This quick exchange would gain humor from the visual language of action and facial expression:

TYB: Why! were ye not served there as ye are,
    Standyng by the fyre chafyng the waxe?
JOHAN [*aside*]: Lo, here be many tryfyls and knakks—
    By kokkis soule, they wene I am other dronke or mad!
TYB: And had ye no meate, Johan Johan? no had?
JOHAN: No, Tyb my wyfe, I had not a whyt.
TYB: What, not a morsel?   JOHAN: No, not one byt.
    For honger, I trowe, I shall fall in a swone.
SIR J: O, that were pyte, I swere by my crowne.
TYB: But is it trewe?   JOHAN: Ye, for a surete.
TYB: Dost thou ly?   JOHAN: No, so mote I the.
TYB: Hast thou had nothyng?   JOHAN: No, not a byt.

TYB: Hast thou not dronke?　JOHAN: No, not a whyt.
TYB: Where wast thou?　JOHAN: By the fyre I dyd stande.
TYB: What dydyst?

(ll. 620-34)

Johan Johan finally explodes, flings the pail to the floor, and
chases Tyb and Sir Johan from the house. The contest for
mastery is in Heywood's farce twofold—physical and mental.
(We note that in *The Pardoner and the Friar* the mental contest
is a draw, but the physical contest is an overwhelming victory for
the knaves.) Tyb and Sir Johan have eaten the pie, the symbol
of their amorous dallying, and have fooled the innocent Johan
Johan. Although he now triumphs physically, the victory is
both momentary and empty. Johan Johan closes the play on this
point; once again Heywood allows dramatic instinct to conquer
didactic tendencies for the play ends on a human note. Johan's
last speech is surely in character:

> A! syrs! I have payd some of them even as I lyst.
> They have borne many a blow with my fyst.
> I thank God, I have walkyd them well,
> And dryven them hens. But yet, can ye tell
> Whether they be go? For, by God, I fere me
> That they be gon together, he and she,
> Unto his chamber; and perhappys she wyll,
> Spyte of my hart, tary there styll;
> And, peradventure, there he and she
> Wyll make me cokold, evyn to anger me.
> And then had I a pyg in the woyrs panyer!
> Therfore, by God, I wyll hye me thyder
> To se yf they do me any vylany.
> And thus, fare well this noble company!

(ll. 665-78)

The defeated go off triumphant, and Johan Johan exists chasing
them. The unity is excellent; there are no loose ends to tie
together.

All six plays were probably performed at court or in the
banquet hall of a lord. The settings are always extremely simple;
Johan Johan demands props but only a trestle and board.
Weather, the most elaborate of the six plays, must have some
sort of throne and curtain to which Jupiter can retire. Since no
other play has more than four parts, *Weather* is also unique
in that it demands ten players; doubling of parts is not possible
since all the petitioners must appear before Jupiter in the

final scene. Furthermore, *Weather* has two female parts and one boy "the lest that can play." I think we can connect *Weather* most closely with a boy's company of actors. Perhaps Heywood wrote it on a special occasion.

The three farces have, as David Bevington has suggested, some of the characteristics of popular drama.[35] It is doubtful if *Johan Johan* was intended for a children's group. It was obviously performed indoors—note especially the audience participation episode where a member of the audience is too close to the door—but *Johan Johan* would be equally appropriate in the repertory of the wandering acting troupes, as would *The Four PP* and perhaps *The Pardoner and the Friar.*

We can suggest one specific place where Heywood's plays might have been performed. Around 1524 John Rastell purchased some land in Finsbury Fields where he built a house and stage. It is not unlikely that on that stage the plays of his son-in-law John Heywood were performed. Little is known of this stage except the reference to it in a court case between John Rastell and a Henry Walton, who constructed the stage, over some damaged garments. Although Walton was forced to pay a court judgment for using various players' garments belonging to Rastell without permission and for failing to replace them when they were damaged, he offered a "counter-claim for 40s. balance of a bill for 50s. costs 'in making of stage for player in Restall's grounde beside Fyndesbury, in tymbre, bourde, nayle, lath, sprigge and other thyngs.' "[36] Both Rastell and Heywood could have seen their plays acted on this stage.

CHAPTER 4

Sources

HEYWOOD, alone of the early sixteenth-century dramatists, reached across the channel both to borrow and translate from the French drama of the period. Any assessment of Heywood's contribution to later drama must recognize his discovery of and dependence upon French farce. That no one followed his lead is one reason for the individuality of his three farces. In many ways he seems closer to the Elizabethans than to the interlude writers of his period, yet his influence upon the Elizabethan drama has been overestimated. He is no more than a minor tributary of the mainstream of the dramatic development. That he produced the best plays in the early part of the century has resulted in his being assigned an undeserving prominence in the development of the later theater. Heywood looks back to Chaucer, not forward to Shakespeare. He is in the native tradition, but he combines the tradition with French farce and thus simultaneously separates himself from the developing indigenous drama.[1]

The relationship of early plays to later Elizabethan drama is a complex one. An interesting lesson can be gained from a quick glance at *Cambises*, which was written by Thomas Preston around 1560, but was still being performed or at least read at the turn of the century. Every reader of Shakespeare is familiar with Falstaff's parodying of the old play: "Give me a cup of sack to make my eyes look red, that it may be thought I have wept; for I must speak in passion, and I will do it in King Cambyses' vein" (*I Henry IV.* II, iv, 422-26). But there is also an artistic connection between such a hybrid morality and the history plays of Shakespeare. *Cambises* is a combination of two disparate actions: the historical story of Cambises, king of Persia, and the plottings of Ambidexter, the vice. If Ambidexter were eliminated, the play would be a historical interlude. But, merely by integrating the vice scenes more effectively into the

108

story and substituting real personages for abstractions, a writer could transform hybird morality into chronicle. The line from *Cambises* to the Henry plays is, therefore, discernible.

Yet another development from the same type of play—the labyrinthine romances, such as the anonymous *Common Conditions* and *Sir Clyomon and Sir Clamydes*—is merely an interesting dramatic phenomenon. These two tedious plays are seldom read outside the scholar's study, for they offer neither entertainment nor the excitement of sources. Heywood's plays still offer entertainment, but are neither sources for, nor important influences upon, the later drama. To deny their influence upon later theater is not any attempt to remove them from their rightful position in Tudor drama. They are important manifestations of Tudor tastes and dramatic abilities and can still elicit laughter.

It is difficult to say why Heywood's plays influenced no later writers. His debates, of course, were a part of a medieval tradition, but his farces surely opened new possibilities. *Johan Johan* is an excellent example of farce, but it stands alone in early Tudor England. The religious controversies of the late 1520's may be one reason for the unique status of *Johan Johan*. Once the split with Rome was final, the interlude was used for polemical purposes; and farce is not suited for controversy. Why Heywood stopped writing is another difficult question. The lost play "Of the parts of Man" was written as late as 1545; the play may mark Heywood's return to a form he had earlier abandoned, but there is little evidence of either subsequent or intervening attempts. To write a debate after producing *Johan Johan*, Heywood must have realized that the times were no longer appropriate for such farces. Why Cranmer asked the Catholic Heywood to write this play is a question that can not be answered from available material. We can only conjecture that Heywood's recantation was believable and acceptable, and that Cranmer then approached a convert whose name might add prestige to the Protestant cause.

The followers of Heywood regarded him as a mad, merry wit, as a writer of epigrams and an entertainer, and not necessarily as a dramatist. They looked back to his jokes, his droll poems—not to his plays. But, if we are to insist upon a dramatic influence, it must be in Heywood's realistic treatment of his characters. For the first time the English stage is

populated by real men and women—Tyb, Johan Johan, Sir Johan
—and not until William Stevenson's *Gammer Gurton's Needle*
(1553) is such a penetration of real life again evident. But any
claim for influence here must be tenuous. Surely the farcical
situations in some Elizabethan drama remind us of the plays of
Heywood, but there is no thread to connect the two. Heywood
is in one sense before his time, and we can easily explain this
later realistic farce as a natural development of both the native
tradition and a new awareness of surrounding life.

Alfred W. Pollard has offered a perceptive comment upon
Heywood's position: ". . . on the subsequent development of
comedy his influence was certainly of the smallest. But to have
shown that comedy was entitled to a separate existence, apart
from didactics, was no small achievement, and to the credit of
this demonstration Heywood is entitled."[2] In this achievement
Heywood may be linked with Chaucer, his master from whom
he borrowed freely; Heywood continues a tradition of perceptive
analysis and poignant satire.

I *The Debates*

A study of Heywood's sources helps to assess his position in
Tudor dramatic literature. His debates, of course, are a continuation of a medieval form and are limited in dramatic possibilities. In *Weather* he extends the form as far as it may go; no
other writer improves upon the genre. No definite source has
been found for any of these three plays, although the French
Dyalogue du fol et du sage, a debat may have influenced *Witty
and Witless*. The differences between the two works, however,
are as striking as the similarities. Since the subject interested
his contemporaries—some of Heywood's ideas parallel passages
in Erasmus' *Encomium Moriae*—it is best to regard *Witty* as a
product of Heywood's imaginative handling of current ideas.
"If he did take something from the *Dialogue*, it was little more
than the title could tell him. The farce was, if anything, the
occasion rather than the source of his play."[3]

The spirit of the French play is, however, far different. There
are only two disputants in the French debate, and they represent
initially a carefree, unconventional Bohemianism and a concern
for wealth, appearances, and status. At first the fool presents
the various advantages of being a fool: little is expected of him;
he is not blamed for his failures. But the central argument is

that he does not have the cares and worries that accompany wealth and position. The dispute centers around wealth, and at the halfway point of the play an identification of wisdom and wealth is made. The French play is not an argument over intelligence; it discusses instead the advantages and disadvantages of money, property, and reputation. By the end of the play it is clear that "le sage" had been living under a false set of values. Le Fol first crystallizes the issue:

> Tu conclus donques que richesse
> Est la sagesse de ce monde?
> Je prie à Dieu qu'il me confonde
> Si ce n'est une folye pure.
> Ostez, ostez; je n'en ay cure:
> Ce n'est que tourment et travail,
> Tantost à pied, puis à cheval.
> Ceste sagesse ne vault rien.
>
> (ll. 315-22)

(You conclude therefore that wealth is the wisdom of the world? I pray to God that it confuses me if this is not pure madness. Away, away; I have no care. This is only torment and travail, sometimes by foot, sometimes by horse. This wisdom is worth nothing.)

The key to the play is the various biblical exhortations against a reliance upon worldly wealth: store up treasures in heaven not on earth. The fool puts it more bluntly: "Car si d'argent tu faitz ton maistre, / Je te tiens pour homme damné" (ll. 580-81). (Because if you make silver your master, I hold you for a man damned.) Finally Le Sage sees his error and confesses that anyone who places his trust in wealth faces a grave danger. (Car je voy qu'il y à danger / De mettre son cueur en richesse [ll. 604-5]). It is extremely unlikely that *Le Dyalogue du Fol et du Sage* is any more than a contemporary analogue, but there may be a lost French play that inspired Heywood. The spirit of Heywood's play is that of Christian humanism. The intelligent man through his good deeds assures himself of a lofty position in heaven. *Le Dyalogue* has a religious emphasis, but has none of the humanistic concern for intelligence. The French play questions false values, but they are those of materialism.

Similarly with *Love* and *Weather* no definite source is available; *Love*, however, handles, as we have noted, a problem of current interest both in Tudor England and on the Continent and a subject that continually engaged writers throughout the century. We can easily assume that Heywood was drawing upon his own experiences and upon the topics and conversations of the More circle. As Bolwell points out, "there is no lack of material for this 'courtly love' of argument."[4] It is easy to see Lover-not-beloved and Beloved-not-loving as the representations of the knight and lady of courtly-love tradition. But Heywood does very skillfully add two other disputants, the other possibilities of the love relationship.

Weather, too, should be seen as an imaginative reworking of contemporary ideas. The theme—the ever-present problem of the weather—is a perfect vehicle for his didactic message and might have easily come to mind, although several sources have been suggested, Lucian's "Icaromenippus" being the most likely—if a source is necessary.[5] Since More published a Latin translation of some of Lucian's *Dialogues* in 1506, Heywood may have known the brief incident recorded in "Icaromenippus" in which Jupiter is hearing the sundry prayers and petitions for his aid. Several contradictory petitions concern the weather: one sailor prayed for a north wind, another for a south wind; farmers prayed for rain; laundrymen for sunshine. If this passage is Heywood's source, we can only admire his imaginative handling and expansion of a very simple idea. To take the one idea that laundrymen were praying for sunshine and to develop the conflict between the Gentlewoman and the Laundress is a mark of Heywood's ability.

Lucian has also been suggested as a possible inspiration for the Pardoner's lie in *The Four PP*,[6] but the story of Menippus' descent to Hades has none of the details of Heywood's tale. It is futile to draw any extended analysis of the two journeys, for Heywood makes no obvious use of Lucian. That both describe a descent into Hell is not sufficient basis for suggesting a source.

II   *The Farces*

If the debates are Heywood's reworking of contemporary ideas, the farces plunge us into the problem of sources. *The Four PP* and *The Pardoner and the Friar* may both be indebted to a French play, *Farce nouvelle d'un Pardonneur, d'un Triacleur, et d'une Taverniere*, as well as to Chaucer. It is in these two plays that Heywood attempts to yoke his natural comic bent with a French form. Yet as Ian Maxwell has pointed out,[7] the French farce is by no means the sole source; for only one character, the Pardoner, appears in both plays; it is quite evident, moreover, that Heywood's pardoners are much more closely related to Chaucer's Pardoner. Yet the French farce is important as an analogue, for Heywood's *The Pardoner and the Friar* is more akin to the French farce than to any other English play.

The French play is short (some 300 lines) and simple. The Pardoner and a Triacleur (a vendor of sundry potions, who corresponds to the Pothecary in Heywood's *The Four PP*) alternate between offering their wares to the audience and ridiculing each other. They are reconciled before they come to blows and enter a tavern at the invitation of the tavern-maid. When they depart, they leave behind a token of thanks, a pair of soiled breeches. The play ends with the discovery by the tavern-maid that what she expected to be a "noble relique" is a pair of breeches.

The vast differences between the plays make it impossible to argue for the French work as a source. Heywood's rivalry in *The Pardoner and the Friar* is between two clerics, a rivalry which ends in reconciliation and a physical beating of the curate and Neighbor Pratt. Nor could one make a sufficient case for *The Four PP* which does share two of its four characters with the French farce. Yet the type is the same, especially in *The Pardoner and the Friar* where basic structure is similar: character A addresses himself to the audience; character B interrupts and then the two fall into verbal attacks upon each other while still attempting to foist their frauds upon the audience. The two villains are reconciled and trick character C. We could argue for the subtlety of the breeches over mere physical abuse, but Heywood draws his play to an effective visual and farcical ending.

There is an obvious concentration or focus in this formula that the more digressive interludes never attain. Even *The Four PP*—although in its central episode it achieves this concentration—has a false start and a painfully didactic moral ending, two features that are incompatible with the essence of farce. For the one salient feature of farce is brevity—a concentration upon a single; realistic incident from ordinary life and the quick destruction of the dramatic illusion with rollicking laughter. There is incidental satire—the anonymous

French writer subjects both the Pardoner and the Triacleur to biting attacks, and Heywood ridicules the pretensions of his two clerics, but the movement of farce is concentrated upon the final turn—the physical beating, the tavern-maid standing with the soiled breeches. Farce elicits uproarious, unthinking laughter; it amuses, it entertains, it never teaches. In *The Pardoner and the Friar* Heywood entertains; he supplements the banquet meal with a penetrating exposé of two rogues, but in the tradition of farce they are humorously victorious. As in real life, the innocent are unwilling, if naïve, victims.

The order of the two plays is still difficult to determine, but it is clear that *The Pardoner and the Friar* is more closely related to the French play. Ian Maxwell would argue that this fact indicates that the farce preceded the more digressive *The Four PP*: "There is every reason to think that in *Four PP* Heywood merely took one or two suggestions from a farce which had served as a model for *Pardoner and Friar*." ". . . we may fairly assume that the germ of it [*The Four PP*] came from *Pardonneur*, passing through a stage of incubation in *Pardoner and Friar*."[8]

Such an argument must, however, be viewed with caution. The one incident in *The Four PP* that could have been borrowed from the French farce is the display of wares by the Pardoner and Pothecary (ll. 482-645). Yet there is nothing in his play for which we can find an actual source in the French play. We must always allow for the possibility of a lost French farce, for we must remember the experience of critics with the source of *Johan Johan*. All conjecture about Heywood's handling of *Pernet* is meaningless now that the actual source has been discovered.

I would suggest that Heywood may have had *Pardonneur* in mind when he wrote *The Four PP*, but used it only incidentally, if at all, in writing the episode of the display of relics. He recognized then or later, however, the dramatic possibilities of French farce. *Pardonneur* is an excellent example of farce, and two of Heywood's plays—*The Pardoner and the Friar* and *Johan Johan* —offer an adequate definition of farce: a short play based upon a realistic, often indecent incident, the sole purpose of which is to amuse. Such a definition can be applied to no other Tudor plays. Heywood thus saw in this play or some other French play a different vehicle for his satirical point and developing dramatic abilities.

If he used the *Pardonneur,* he made two important changes—
the Triacleur became a friar and a tavern-maid became the
parson and Neighbor Pratt; only the structure remained the same.
The possibility that there is a lost French farce similar to
Heywood's play is a strong one, since such changes are drastic
ones. However, *The Pardoner and the Friar* exemplifies French
farce; it is a dramatic whole with no digression or extraneous
material. It manifests dramatic skill and realism that the other
plays had only suggested. *Johan Johan,* on the other hand, is
French farce.

Johan Johan is a translation of a French farce; and critics,
as we have noted, had formerly suggested a parallel in *De
Pernet qui va au vin.*[9] But T. W. Craik has convincingly proved
that Heywood's play is a close translation of *Farce nouvelle et
fort joyeuse du Paste et est a trois personnaiges. C'est assavoir:
l'Homme, la Femme, le Cure.*[10] We can select at random in the
farce to demonstrate Heywood's dependence upon his source:

> Yet I almost enrage that I ne can
> Se the behavour of our gentylwoman.
> And yet, I thynke, thyther as she doth go,
> Many an honest wyfe goth thyther also. . .
>
> (ll. 89-92)

> J'enrage presque je ne puis
> Veoir le tour de nostre bourgeoise
> Et aufort je prens qu'elle y voyse.
> Plusieurs femmes de bien y vont.
>
> (ll. 91-94)

But Heywood is not always this literal. For instance, the entry of
the wife is more effective in Heywood's version. Tyb enters
during Johan's monologue, immediately taking the offensive:

> TYB: Why, whom wylt thou beate, I say, thou knave?
> JOHAN: Who, I, Tyb? None, so God me save.
> TYB: Yes, I harde the say thou woldest one bete.
> JOHAN: Mary, wyfe, it was stokfysshe in Temmes Strete,
> Whiche wyll be good meate agaynst Lent.
> Why, Tyb, what haddest thou thought that I
> had ment?
> TYB: Mary, me-thought I harde the bawlyng.
> Wylt thou never leve this wawlyng?
> Howe the dyvell dost thou thy selfe behave?
> Shall we ever have this worke, thou knave?

JOHAN: What! wyfe, howe sayst thou? was it well
    gest of me,
That thou woldest be come home in safete
As soon as I had kendled a fyre?
Come warme the, swete Tyb, I the requyre.

(ll. 111-24)

From what follows, we know Heywood has expanded the following exchange; La Femme enters with the pie:

Et dont vous vient ceste murmure,
Ferez-vous jamais que tanser?
Que dyable avez-vous à crier?
Hau! Jehan-Jehan, vous faut-il rien?

L'HOMME:
Mais ne le disoye pas bien
Que vostre corps seroit venu
Avant que j'eusse esprins le feu.
Or vous venez chauffer ma mye!

(ll. 119-26)

Heywood also makes some interesting changes even when he is
translating very closely; the French version of Tyb's defense
of her lover reads thus:

J'entens bien comment
Vous vous doubtez, mais c'est à tort.
Morte soye de male mort
Se ce n'est ung vray catholicque.

(ll. 239-42)

Heywood embellishes the final idea:

Mary, I perceyve very playne
That thou hast Syr Johan somwhat in suspect;
But, by my soule, as far as I conject,
He is vertuouse and full of charyte.

(ll. 229-32)

It would be futile to list all of Heywood's changes since the
important point is that he has translated directly from a French
farce. But Heywood does give the French play an English
flavor. Where the French version only suggests the *fabliau*
humor, Heywood presses the point.

L'HOMME:
Ha! curé que Dieu le vous rende,
Je suis trop tenu à vous.

LE CURE:
Qu'elle ne soit nette devant vous
Et de son corps femme de bien,
Si est.

L'HOMME:
Je n'ay doubté de rien,
Dieu mercy, et vostre doctrine.
Pourroye savoir la racine
Du debat entre vous et elle?

(ll. 365-72)

JOHAN:
Now God yeld it yow, god master curate,
And as ye do, so send you your helth.
Ywys, I am bound to you a plesure.

SYR JOHAN:
Yet thou thynkyst amys, peradventure,
That of her body she shuld not be a good woman.
But I shall tell the what I have done, Johan,
For that matter; she and I be somtyme aloft,
And I do lye uppon her many a tyme and oft
To prove her; yet could I never espy
That ever any dyd worse with her than I.

JOHAN:
Syr, that is the lest care I have of nyne,
Thankyd be God, and your good doctryne.
But, yf it please you, tell me the matter,
And the debate betwene you and her.

(ll. 343-56)

Heywood does not always improve upon his sources. The introduction of the priest's miracles is much more appropriate in the French farce. There the tales follow dramatically upon the husband's overheard aside, which he tries to cover by claiming that he was attempting to remember an illustration from last Sunday's sermon:

L'HOMME:
Comment il fourre sa besasse!
Que estrangler puist-il du pasté!

LA FEMME:
Or nous raconte verité,
Qu'esse que tu dis, par ton âme?

L'HOMME:
Par bieu je comptoye, ma femme,
À par moy, en chauffant la cire,
Une exemple que j'ouy dire
À nostre curé dimenche au soir,
Mais ce n'est pas à mon povoir
Que je le sceusse retrouver.

LA FEMME:
Vous plairoit-il de nous compter
Quelque compte honneste pour rire?

L'HOMME:
Entant que je chauffe la cire,
Grant plaisir prens de le savoir.

                                        (ll. 573-86)

The priest then moves easily into the telling of his three miracles.
By ignoring Johan Johan's aside, Heywood forces Tyb to make a
painfully obvious request for after dinner entertainment: "Now
Master Parson, pleasyth your goodnes / To tell us some tale of
myrth or sadnes / For our pastyme, in way of communycacyon?"
(ll. 529-31). As Professor Craik has pointed out, Heywood's
translation of the three miracles is very free.[11]

But the important change in the play is in the ending where
Heywood demonstrates his acute dramatic sense. The ending
of the French farce employs physical action, but the humor
and poignancy of the short-lived victory of Johan Johan are
absent. The last speech, when Johan Johan stands alone on the
stage, begins with a triumphant cry, "A! syrs! I have payd some
of them even as I lyst. / They have borne many a blow with my
fyst" (ll. 665-66); but it ends with the doubts and anxieties of
a cuckolded husband. In the French version the husband also
wins a battle, but the inner turmoil is neither mentioned nor
resolved:

L'HOMME:
    Vive Sainct George!
À ly! à ly! a! maistre prestre,
Vuyder vous feray de cest estre,
Vous en aures, tenez, tenez,
Nostre pasté mangé avez,
Mais il vous sera chier vendu,
À force vous verray vaincu,
Or sus, or sus à ly! à ly!

LA FEMME:
À ly! cure!

L'HOMME:
  Je vous vy
À! vous estes trop contre moy,
À! par le corps bieu, je m'en voys
Et y garde ce qui vouldra.

LA FEMME:
Par où s'en va-il?

LE CURÉ
  Par dela!
Je vous pry, suyvons- le de près.
L'homme revient par derrière
  atout ung sac plain de pain.
Après curé, après, après.
À! vous me gastés le pasté,
Après, curé, après, curé,
À ly! à ly à ly! à ly!
Or, Messeigneurs, adieu vous dy!
                              (ll. 749-67)

The French farce then ends with a typical farcical beating, but
Heywood recognizes fully the possibilities of Johan Johan's
character and the futility of his violence. I think this change is
an extremely important one. In many ways farce depends upon
shallow characterization, a two-dimensional figure; and Johan
Johan is treated two dimensionally in the French play. But
Heywood adds the third dimension; the mental conflict comple-
ments the physical conflict.

Though we can praise the changes Heywood made while
translating and emphasize how he had made the play seem so
native that scholars had never suspected that he might be
merely translating a foreign play, we must finally reassess
Heywood's contribution to drama. His best play is not his own
but a foreign play. In three plays he successfully combines his
own skill with the form of farce, but he does not continue to
explore the obvious possibilities. Heywood's dramatic reputation
rests, therefore, on these six plays.

CHAPTER 5

John Heywood and Tudor Drama

I   Gentleness and Nobility

WE should glance briefly at the surrounding drama in early sixteenth-century England in order to emphasize Heywood's position in this period; and we must start with *Gentleness and Nobility*,[1] a debate which has occasionally been credited to our author. On the one side stand Bolwell, Kenneth Cameron, and Tucker-Brooke arguing for Heywood as the author. Cameron, the most persuasive spokesman for this group, must admit that no definite statement is possible:

> Summarizing our results, we find (1) that verbal parallels are often of doubtful value in establishing authorship of a Tudor play when it is derived, like *Gentleness*, from commonplaces; (2) that *Gentleness* contains rare humor, keenly enjoyable to the Court circle; (3) that its author had a sense of proportion; (4) that the epilogue is probably Rastell's chief contribution to the piece, although his *Four Elements* may have supplied the author with several ideas; (5) that the More-Rastell-Heywood circle read much the same literature—to be found, probably, in More's library—and cooperated through a liberal exchange of opinions; (6) that Heywood is not an impossible candidate for *Gentleness*.[2]

Wallace, however, assigns the play to Cornish; and Esther Dunn, Frederick Boas, and A. W. Reed argue for the authorship of John Rastell. Esther Dunn speaks for this contingent: "In the light of the remarkable accord of the subject of *Gentleness and Nobility* with Rastell's pronounced ideals; and in the light of the very different attitudes which seem to set off our author from the Heywood of *Wit and Folly*; and especially in the close connexion and even identical usage of words in which *Gentleness and Nobility* parallels the *Four Elements*. Rastell's authorship of *Gentleness and Nobility* seems to be a safe probability.[3] It should be mentioned that Francis Kirkman in 1671 had listed separately the two parts of *Gentleness and Nobility,* as well as the other five printed plays—*Witty* was still in manuscript—with John Heywood as author.[4]

The problems of anonymous plays in Tudor England should warn critics about making rash assignments. Even when the author is given, disputes about his identity may arise. An excellent example is the authorship of *Cambises.* The name on the title page is Thomas Preston; but who is Thomas Preston, an itinerant playwright or the academic at Cambridge College who also wrote Latin poems? And did the playwright, whoever he is, also write the broadside ballads that appeared in the 1570's? The point is that no definitive statement can be made about the authorship of most anonymous plays.

The problem with *Gentleness and Nobility* is that we have little external evidence to support internal conjectures which may be liable to bias because of the point of view with which we approach the play. The colophon which has been cited in assigning the play to Rastell—"Johannes Rastell me fieri fecit"—is too ambigious to use as proof of authorship; it may merely refer to Rastell as the publisher. It is unusual, however, that Rastell did not give his son-in-law's name if Heywood was indeed the author. Yet the play is prefaced by the same woodcut of, I assume, John Heywood that prefaces the editions of *The Spider and the Fly.* The initials below the man are I. H., which suggest John Heywood; the presence of the woodcut is a mystery if Heywood is not the author; for, if the cutting is not of Heywood, how does one explain its appearance in *The Spider and the Fly,* the authorship of which is not in dispute?

The strongest internal evidence for Heywood's authorship is the prosody and the similarity of the Plowman's argument for gentility with that of the old hag in the "Wife of Bath's Tale."[5] J. E. Bernard argues that his study of the versification strengthens the possibility that Heywood is the author of the play.[6] The dominant meter is tetrameter couplets, but the author also employs a small percentage of tetrameter rhyme royal. After admitting this point, we must recognize that the play reflects common Tudor ideas, concepts shared by More, Heywood, Rastell, and other writers of the period.

In *Fulgens and Lucrece,* Henry Medwall has two suitors present the arguments for gentility and birth and gentility and worth. This dramatizing of a common idea then means that the

diligent searcher will find parallels not only with Heywood's
plays and most obviously with *The Spider and the Fly,* the
poem in which Heywood is most concerned with contemporary
social problems, but also with John Rastell's *Four Elements* and
some of his prose writings, *Pastyme of People* and *Boke of Purgatory.* To argue from one or two such similarities ignores the
problem of this genre. Not only could either Rastell or Heywood
have written this play, but other writers who shared this common
bond could be advanced as candidates.[7] Furthermore, it is
entertainment for an audience that would understand and
appreciate the arguments, not a presentation of a unique or
controversial subject or point of view.

One last example of the confusion, and I will then turn to
the play itself. The epilogue is spoken in rhyme royal by a
philosopher, whereas the rest of the play is in the usual couplets.
Two points have been mentioned about this epilogue. *Love,
Witty,* and *Weather* all end with sections in rhyme royal; thus
one can argue that Heywood here ends *Gentleness* in a similar
fashion to his other debates. Yet Rastell frequently employs
rhyme royal in *The Four Elements,* and Kenneth Cameron has
argued that the Philosopher's speech is Rastell's addition to
Heywood's play.[8] The point should be evident: we can make
only tentative comments about authorship.

Including *Gentleness and Nobility* in the Heywood canon
does not change Heywood's position in early Tudor drama. The
play fits rather neatly with *Witty* and *Love;* the author here
handles three actors with some dramatic skill. There is an
occasionally lively exchange that often seems to capture the
flavor of actual conversation. The play, which is divided into
two parts, opens with the Merchant's boasting about his contributions to the commonwealth; he is joined by the Knight and
the argument centers around gentility. The Knight lists his
criteria for a gentleman: "Mary I call them gentylmen that be
/ Born to grete landys by inherytaunce" (434). The Merchant
counters this argument:

> For I call hym a gentylman that gentilly
> Doth gyf unto other men louyngly
> Such thing as he hath of hys own proper
> But he that takith ought away from a nother
> And doth gyf hym no thyng agayn therfore
> Owght to be callyd a chorle euermore.
>
> (435)

The egoism of the two disputants reminds one of the Gentleman and Merchant of *Weather*. In fact, the philosophies of the Gentleman and the Knight and the two Merchants are so similar that the characters are almost interchangeable. When *Gentleness and Nobility* opens with the Merchant's boast that any kingdom that has merchants has wealth and prosperity, we recall the Merchant in *Weather* prefacing his appeal to Jupiter with this plea: "Fyrste to consyder the desert of our request, / What welth we bryng the rest, to our great care and stryfe, / And then to rewarde us as ye shall thynke best" (ll. 350-52).

The Knight then argues that his ancestors were wiser than the Merchant's, a claim that the Merchant vehemently denies. The Knight boasts of wise judges and courageous warriors; the Merchant brags of skillful artisans. Bursting with pride, the Knight sums up his argument, not knowing that the Plowman, the third disputant, is listening. The technique of sharply penetrating their pretensions through comic contrast is evident in this exchange. The Knight is speaking:

> Therefore consyderyng my grete lynage
> By blode my noble byrth and parentage
> Thou art not able to compare with me
> Nother in gentylnes nor in nobylyte.
> *Here the plowman commith in with a short whyp*
> *in hys hand & spekyth as folowith*
> Now here is bybbyll babbyll clytter clatter
> I hard neuer of so folysh a matter
> But by goddys body to speke the troth
> I am better than other of you bothe.
>
> (439)

When the Plowman attacks the assumption that nobility is a result of birth, he echoes the thinking of the More circle on true nobility: "And of the acts that your auncestours did before / ye ar the nobler neuer the more" (440). Henry Medwall in *Fulgens and Lucrece* had earlier put similar thoughts into the mouth of Gayus Flaminius; he is answering Fulgens, who had boasted of his ancestor's deeds:

> Fyrst of your auncetours ye allege the noble gestis,
> Secondly the substance that ye haue of theyr bequestes.
> In the whiche thingis onely by your owne confession
> Standeth all your noblenes, this sayd ye beffore:
> Wherevnto this I say, vnder the correction

Of lucres oure Iugge here, that ye are neuer the more
Worthy in myne oppynion to be callyd noble therefore,
And withoute ye haue better causes to shew than these
Of reson ye must the victory of this matter lese.

                                        (ll. 604-12)

The Plowman proceeds to prove in a fashion his claim to
nobility. He asks if God, being self-sufficient, is not the noblest
of all and then argues that the Plowman, being the most self-
sufficient of the three, is also the noblest: "So suffycyency is
euer noblenes / And necessyte is euer wrechydnes" (443). The
Plowman must then answer the complaint that beasts, having
no need for clothing, are more noble than man. Here he dis-
courses on man's excellent soul which insures his superiority
over the animal world. The Merchant, realizing that he is
defeated, insists that they return to the original subject: Who
is the gentleman? In the first part of the play two commonplace
Tudor ideas are explored: the relationship between birth and
nobility, and the superiority of man's soul or intellect.

When the Plowman excuses himself to go to market, the
pause in the play allows for some lighter entertainment before
the three disputants return. The second half centers around the
justice of landed property and inheritance. The Knight claims
that the lands and rents were given to his ancestors because
of their virtues and gentleness. Prior to this class division there
were constant wars and rebellions because all attempted to
increase their wealth. The Plowman's historical perspective is
far different:

> By goggs swete body thou lyest falsely
> All possessions began furst of tyranny
> For when people began furst to encrese
> Some gafe themself all to Idylnes
> And wold not labour but take by vyolence
> That other men gat by labour & dylygence.
>   (453)

And we must recognize in the following passage a comment
upon contemporary conditions similar to several details in
Heywood's *The Spider and the Fly*, for *Gentleness and Nobility*
is another of those sundry Tudor works concerned with the
plight of the common people. The Plowman is countering the
Knight's claim that much good comes from the laws of
inheritance:

Nay mych Ill commyth thereof I shall proue how
For these men that be of gret possessyons
Unto theyr blod haue such affeccyons
Yf any land lyke them that lyeth nye them
Of theyr pore neghbors they wyll distroy them
Or by extort meanys they wyll them compell
The land for half the worth to them to sell
And when they lake money they wyl alwey
Euer borow & neuer wyllyng to pay
And when they shall dye ye see thexpience
Few of them haue remors of consyens
To make any maner restytucyon
Of any land so wrongfully gotton.

(454-55)

The Knight then demonstrates that we have moved from the stage to the lecture room. He asks what the Plowman thinks of merchants, and the Plowman launches his attack against the corrupt merchants, allowing, however, that many are virtuous and just.

Finally the Knight can no longer control his anger; the Merchant must prevent a fight between the Plowman and Knight. This abortive struggle is the only indication of any stage action and offers a welcome break in the monotony. The Plowman then advances his own solution to the problem: that there should be no inheritance, but that the rulers of the land should possess property and benefit from the labor of others. Only those who work for the good of the commonwealth deserve to possess property. Those who think only of their descendants should not be allowed to rule or to hold land. Furthermore, estates should be held only for the term of the owner's life: "And such people of vertuouse condycyons / And no nother shuld be chosyn gouernours / & thei shuld haue lands to maintain their honours" (459).

If Heywood is the author of this play, a slight re-evaluation of Heywood should be made. I said before that Heywood is not an original thinker or philosopher, but this section on inheritance is more obviously political and philosophical than anything we find in Heywood's other plays. Rastell, who elsewhere demonstrated his philosophical interests, may be a more likely candidate for the authorship of such passages.

The Merchant again insists on returning to the original subject, but the disputants are unable to reach any solution. The

Plowman, alone on stage briefly before the other two re-enter,
sums up the author's intention; for the play not only satirizes
the pretensions of all three figures, but makes a disguised social
comment:

> Wee see well now by playne expience
> When a man is set in a wyllfull credens
> All to fortefye hys owne opynyon
> If god hym selfe than wold wyth hym reason
> In effect it shall no more auayle
> Than w+ a whyp to dryfe a snayle
> Therfore no remedy is that I can see
> For yuell men that be in auctoryte
> But let them alone tyll god wyll send
> A tyme tyll our gouernours may intend
> Of all enormytes the reformacyon.

(466)

The Plowman returns to his plow while the Knight and the
Merchant enter to disparage their opponent and present the
advantages of inherited rule; they can agree that they are
superior to the Plowman and fortunately do not renew their
original argument. The play seems complete when the two
disputants leave the stage, but an unannounced philosopher
enters to deliver a lengthy, didactic epilogue; and that the play
was intended to educate the ruling classes is indicated by
references to the sovereigns watching the play.

The Philosopher announces the actual criterion for gentility:
"The thyng that makyth a gentylman to be / ys but vertew &
gentyll condycyons / whych as well in pore men oft tymys
we se / As in men of grete byrth or hye degre" (470). He
briefly discusses nobility, which also depends upon virtue, not
entirely upon self-sufficiency. Finally, he comments upon "who
shulde be chose to hye auctoryte," emphasizing again that only
the virtuous should rule. There is only a passing reference to the
Plowman's theory of inheritance: "And in auctoryte they ought
not contynue / Except they be good men dyscrete & wyse"
(471). The Philosopher concludes with a few comments on the
necessity of just laws, a subject which was only briefly
mentioned in the play itself.

Some clue to the authorship may be hidden in the last few
lines:

And though that I my selfe now percase
Thus myn oppynyon haue publyshed
Or any of my felowes here in this place
In any poynt here haue vs abused
We beseche you to holde vs excused
And so the auctour hereof requyreth you all
And thus I commyt you to god eternall.

A M E N

Johens rastell me fieri fecit.

(472)

Does the Philosopher still speak these last lines, or has the mask been dropped? It is possible that Rastell is speaking here, referring to the epilogue that he has just penned and to another man as the author of the play. But such speculation finds no proof. Rastell, of course, could be referring to himself as author, or the Philosopher may still be speaking—and the last idea is the most likely possibility. The Philosopher then refers to his own hand in the epilogue, apologizes for any tactless passages, and mentions the anonymous author's wish.

Since no final statement can be made, it is safer to treat the play as a work of unknown authorship. We cannot dismiss the possibility of an anonymous playwright; for, since the play dramatizes Tudor commonplaces, any argument from the continuity of ideas is suspect. We can suggest Heywood as the author, we can fit the play neatly into the Heywood canon, but we cannot be sure; nor is the problem too important. *Gentleness and Nobility* is a play of early Tudor England; it is one part of the development of the drama, but it reflects the times, not the author. Only *The Four PP, The Pardoner and the Friar, Johan Johan,* Rastell's *Calisto and Melibaea,* and Medwall's *Fulgens and Lucrece* stand apart from the normal drama of the Tudor period.

II *Contemporary Drama*

John Rastell is, however, the accepted author of two plays, *Calisto and Melibaea,* a partial translation from the Italian translation of the Spanish *Celistina,* and *The Nature of the Four Elements,* an educational drama. Since *Calisto and Melibaea* is a translation, it does not reflect the native tradition or the educational aspect of the developing interlude. Like Heywood's farces and Medwall's *Fulgens and Lucrece,* it suggests alternate routes that the inchoate drama might have developed along, but did not.

Melibaea, who suggests Heywood's Beloved-not-loving, is pursued by Calisto. She is almost persuaded into acquiescing to his lustful demands by a bawd, Celestina. Her father's timely dream warns her of the fateful consequences of such a decision, and she escapes from this damnation. Her father then presents the dramatically indefensible moral: God will grant mercy to all truly repentant sinners. Rastell sees the play as an exemplum for "virgins and fair maidens all."

The moralistic ending is completely foreign to the spirit of the play itself. Rastell even goes so far as to suggest that the play offers advice to rulers of youth: ". . . your charge is doubtless / To bring them up virtuously, and to see / Them occupied still in some good business; / Not in idle pastime or unthriftiness" (91). We can see in this ending the obvious tension between the story and Rastell's moralistic interpretation. In his other play he is not restricted by another author's story and is able to give full play to his didactic instincts.

Rastell's other play, *The Nature of the Four Elements,* demonstrates the uses to which the interlude was put. After a list of the players, Rastell offers a catalogue of subjects to be covered; and three of the ten subjects are: "Of the situation of the four elements, that is to say, the earth, the water, the air, and fire, and of their qualities and properties, and of the generation and corruption of things made of the commixtion of them. Of certain conclusions proving that the sea lieth round upon the earth. Of the cause of the winds and thunder" (5-6). A play may be an interesting way to teach geography, but it is questionable entertainment for guests. As Ignorance says, in one of those interesting references to the audience:

> For the foolish arguing that thou hast had
> With that knave Experience, that hath made
> All these folk thereof weary;
> For all that they be now in this hall,
> They be the most part my servants all,
> And love principally
> Disports, as dancing, singing,
> Toys, trifles, laughing, jesting;
> For cunning they set not by.
>
> (45-46)

The dancing and singing would offer welcome relief from the lessons about geography and the explanations of the tide that opened the play. Rastell even admitted that his play did not appeal to all tastes; on the title page he says the work will last an hour and a half; "but, if ye list, ye may leave out much of the sad matter, as the Messenger's part, and some of Nature's part, and some of Experience's part, and yet the matter will depend conveniently, and then it will not be past three-quarters of an hour of length."

If we ignore the educational aspect, we find the traditional morality structure; the virtues are Studious Desire and Experience. Sensual Appetite and Ignorance, the vices, corrupt the hero, Humanity. The play can best be classified as an educational or humanistic morality. The final purpose is to bring the auditor to worship God; but the immediate purpose is the advancement of learning, the defeat of ignorance. The Messenger's opening plea for the translation of scientific books into English manifests the humanistic bent of this and other early Tudor plays.

Another, if somewhat later, educational dissertation is John Redford's *Wit and Science.* Again the morality play is transformed for the humanistic goal of secular education. Wit, a young student, wishes to wed Lady Science, whose father is Reason. To win his beloved, he must overcome the monster Tediousness. On one side are aligned the virtues—Instruction, Study, Diligence, Honest Recreation, and Confidence; the opponents are such abstractions as Idleness, Ignorance, and Shame, formidable foes of any student. The lesson of the play is obvious: the young student, who would not only be the protagonist but also the audience, must avoid the various temptations dramatized in Redford's play.

In the student's first attempt, Wit is accompanied only by Study and Diligence; he ignores the warnings of Instruction and is an easy victim before the onslaught of Tediousness. Honest Recreation revives him, but he falls under the influence of Idleness who dresses him in the garb of Ignorance. In this disguise he unknowingly approaches Lady Science who rebukes him. Then discovering his appearance in a mirror, he lapses into despair. He begs another chance from Reason, and once again he is presented to Instruction, Study, and Diligence. This time the four of them subdue Tediousness, and Wit wins the hand of Lady Science amidst much rejoicing.

The songs which enliven the performance suggest that Red-

ford was writing for a children's group. The play is obviously
intended to make palatable the necessity for study and diligence
in education, as Redford dramatizes the traps that confront any
young student. The didactic aspects of the play, however,
overwhelm the dramatic qualities; there are interludes of singing
and dancing, but their connection with the main idea is tenuous.
There are also some humorous stretches that break the monotony
of the author's message. The attempt of Idleness to teach
Ignorance his own name is an example of low verbal play. Of a
higher level is Wit's discovery that he is dressed in a fool's
clothes:

> [*He looks in the glass.*]
> Hah! Goges sowle! What have we here? A dyvyll?
> This glas, I se well, hath bene kept evyll.
> [*Cleans the glass, and looks again.*]
> Goges sowle! a foole! a foole, by the mas!
> What a very vengeance aylth this glas?
> Other this glas is shamefully spotted,
> Or els am I to shamefully blotted!
> Nay, by Goges armes, I am so, no dowte!
> How loke ther facis heere rownd abowte?
> [*He holds the glas up to the audience.*]
> All fayre and cleere, they, evrychone;
> And I, by the mas, a foole alone,
> Deckt, by Goges bones, lyke a very asse!
>
> (ll. 802-12)

We may momentarily not recognize the speaker as Wit, but
Redford does offer a good passage of stage action. The Tudor
dramatist always recognized the audience as more than mere
spectator, as finally a possible actor in the play; and he often
utilized it thus.

Henry Medwall, the chaplain of John Morton, wrote two
plays before the turn of the century that best illustrate the
new dramatic activity. His play *Nature* (before 1500) recounts
in typical morality fashion the temptations and failures of man
until old age convinces him of his folly. But the play is a humanistic morality; the philosophical point of view is Aristotelian:

> But yf ye couet / now to know theffecte
> Of thyngs naturall / by trew conclusyon
> Counsell with Arystotell / my phylosopher electe
> Whyche hath left / in bokys of hys tradycyon
> How euery thyng / by heuynly constellacyon

> Is brought to effecte / and in what maner wyse
> As far as mannys wytt / may naturally compryse.
>
> (ll. 57-63)

Nature instructs Mankind to avoid Sensuality and to follow the guidance of Reason and Innocence; after he exits, Reason and Sensuality argue over their relative importance and eventually bring Mankind to World before whom they continue their dispute. World advises him to shun the company of Reason and Innocence and follow the counsel of Worldly Affection and Sensuality.

The pattern of the morality is established, but the values are more secular than religious in the first part of the play. These vice characters dominate the action as they corrupt Mankind; then Reason is allowed to lament the fall of Mankind and to confront him in an attempt to reconvert him. It is important that Reason's lament does not mention the religious ramifications of Mankind's corruption but emphasizes the bestial existence— "a brute best that lakketh reson" (l. 1306); "suche bestly lyuyng" (l. 1312)—that the Tudors claimed accompanied the absence of reason or wit. As mankind momentarily repents, the first part of the play ends.

The second part of Nature repeats the same pattern. The unity of Reason and Mankind is disturbed, and Mankind cavorts with the Seven Deadly Sins until Old Age convinces him of his folly. This pattern, that of the traditional morality, is in the same mainstream as *Mankind,* a slightly earlier play. The same subject is treated by an anonymous author in *The World and the Child,* printed in 1522. Here Mankind is followed through the various stages of his life, each stage being marked by a new name; from fourteen to twenty-one he is Lust and Liking, and at twenty-one he becomes Manhood Mighty; finally he becomes Age and, in typical morality fashion, laments his past and repents.

The adaptation of the interlude to polemics was a natural concomitant of the religious controversies of Henry's reign. *Hickscorner* (1500-20) defends the Roman Catholic Church by pitting three virtues against three vices and by discarding completely the central figure of most moralities, Mankind. There is some good stage business and an effectively dramatized conflict. *Interlude of Youth* (1513-29) and *Lusty Juventus* (1547-53) show the corruption of youth and support the Catholic and Protestant viewpoints, respectively.

Other Tudor adaptations of the morality must be mentioned; John Skelton's *Magnificence* (1516) replaces the religious emphasis with lessons in the education and moral instruction of a prince. "There is no prince but he hath need of us three: / Wealth with Measure, and pleasant liberty" (170). Magnificence, the name of the prince, is, however, corrupted by such political vices as Fancy, Counterfeit Countenance, and Crafty Conveyance. Finally Magnificence is stripped of all his worldly possessions and contemplates suicide. Goodhope, however, snatches the knife away and returns Magnificence to the way of righteousness. The last part of the play is spent reinforcing the painfully obvious political lesson.

Another artist of the interlude form was John Bale, who wrote several plays that teach religious lessons. In *The Chief Promises of God* (1538) Bale divides his drama into seven acts, in which God successively delivers his covenants to Adam, Noah, Abraham, Moses, David, Isaiah, and John the Baptist. The purpose of the play is to remind the modern man of his duty to God and of the sacrifice of Jesus Christ. Written in 1538, *The Chief Promises of God* and his other interludes—*John Baptistes Preaching in the Wilderness* (1538); *The Temptation of Our Lord by Satan* (1538); *Comedy Concerning Three Laws, of Nature Moses and Christ* (1538)—are the complete opposite of what Heywood had brought to the stage in *The Four PP* and in *Johan Johan*. We can get no better idea of the extremes in Tudor drama than to turn from Heywood to Bale.

In one play Bale combined his Protestant bias with his historical interests. *King John* fluctuates between history and allegory, but it presents at times rather effectively the exploitation of the Widow England at the hands of Rome's clergy and the king's futile efforts to save her and her blind son Commonality. The Pope and his clergy are the undiluted villains of the play, as Bale twists history for polemical purposes. An Interpreter who appears between the two parts of the play connects King John's dispute with the Pope with a more recent religious controversy and of course emphasizes the author's sympathies for the Protestant Reformation:

> This noble Kynge Johan, as a faythfull Moyses,
> Withstode proude Pharo for hys poor Israel,
> Myndynge to brynge yt owt of the lande of darkenesse,
> But the Egyptyanes did agaynst hym so rebell
> That hys poore people ded styll in the desart dwell,
> Tyll that Duke Josue, whych was our late Kynge Henrye,
> Clerely brought us in-to the lande of mylke and honye.
>
>   (ll. 1106-12)

Our purpose in this section is not to trace the subsequent development of the drama but to show that the historical moralities such as *Cambises* and the explications of popular proverbs—*The Longer Thou Livest the More Fool Thou Art, Enough Is As Good As A Feast*—result from the breaking down of the religious emphasis of the old morality play. The structure remains the same, but the themes are different. The point that must be made is that the Tudor dramatists adapted the morality framework to their own political, educational, and polemical interests. The humanists explored new ideas; the playwrights dramatized the current controversies and opened new vistas for dramatic art.

Henry Medwall's second play, *Fulgens and Lucrece*, is based upon *De Vera Nobilitate*, a discourse on nobility by Bonus Accursius and translated into English by John Tiptoft in 1481. It is not, however, a translation, but an original treatment of a subject of interest to the humanists. But, more important to the student of drama, Medwall offers the first comic subplot in English drama.

Lucrece is wooed by two suitors, one rich, the other plain and humble, and eventually chooses the latter. Her maid also must choose between the servingmen of the two suitors and this parody of the wooing is uproariously comic. Lucrece promises to marry the suitor she judges most noble, and the second part of the play contains the suitors' defenses of their own nobility. These passages, of course, remind us of *Gentleness and Nobility* and reflect the contemporary interest in this problem that the hag in the *Wife of Bath's Tale* had earlier discussed. Cornelius, the rich suitor, brags of his possessions, his ancestors, his position, whereas Flaminius stresses the familiar argument that true nobility depends upon worth not birth:

> To the fyrst parte as touching your auncetous dedes
> Some of them were noble lyke as ye declare,
> Thestoris bereth witnes, I must graunt them nedes,
> But yet for all that some of them ware
> Of contrary diposycion like as ye are,
> For they dyde no proffite, no more do ye,
> To the comon wele of this noble cytie.
>
> Yf ye wyll the title of noblenes wynne
> Shew what haue ye done yourself therfore:
> Some of your owne meritis let se bryng in,
> Yf euer ye dyde ony syth ye were bore;

> But surely ye haue no suche thyng in store
> Of your owne merites wherby of right
> Ye shulde appere noble to ony mannys sight.
>
> (ll. 613-26)

Medwall's originality in the handling of the subplot makes *Fulgens and Lucrece* unique in early Tudor drama. But, just as no one followed Heywood's explorations of French farce, no Tudor dramatist adapted the structure of *Fulgens and Lucrece*. But perhaps Medwall's contemporaries were not concerned with the innovative technique of paralleling the main plot with a subplot; instead they found in the second part of *Fulgens and Lucrece* a debate similar to those which Heywood had dramatized. Medwall's audience may have been more interested in the serious debate than in the comic parody of the wooing.

Both of Medwall's plays were written before the turn of the century, and both reflect humanistic thought. In *Nature* Medwall takes an established dramatic structure and turns it to new uses. In *Fulgens and Lucrece* he constructs the first comic subplot in English drama but also utilizes contemporary thinking on true nobility. To praise *Fulgens and Lucrece* over *Nature*, as every modern reader would, ignores the uses of the drama in early Tudor England. As we move through the next few decades, we find no developments from the one, but a continuous stream from *Nature*. The Tudor dramatist was foremost interested in the drama as a vehicle for his ideas; structure and other artistic problems were secondary if they were even considered. Thus such Tudor interludes as *Nature, Wit and Science, The World and the Child, The Four Elements,* and their successors form a convenient unit.

Yet several other plays which manifest simultaneous experimentation are ones that exerted no noticeable influence on the subsequent drama, but they are also important examples of Tudor dramatic abilities. John Heywood is the author of three plays that do not fit conveniently into this pattern of the Tudor interlude. From *The Four PP* to *Johan Johan* we see for the only time in Tudor England the gradual emergence of the play as a unified work. That Heywood was translating from a French farce should not change the estimate of Heywood's contribution; for, in *Johan Johan,* the play itself, not some authorial message, is the thing. In *Fulgens and Lucrece, Calisto,* to some extent in *The Four PP,* and obviously in the other interludes of the period, the author is first humanist or Catholic or Protestant; only second is he a dramatist. In *The Pardoner and the Friar* and *Johan Johan* this tension is absent.

III The Heywood Legacy

To realize the true importance of such experiments, we have to gain historical perspective. To be sure, Heywood and Medwall formed no schools; but they did explore and widen the potentialities of the drama just as William Stevenson in *Gammer Gurton's Needle* and Nicholas Udall in *Ralph Roister Doister* did a few years later. The flowering of all these efforts is the Elizabethan drama which assimilates the native tradition and the foreign elements into a unified whole. Heywood and Medwall very early experimented with some of the elements—realistic humor, comic subplot—we so lavishly praise in Shakespeare and his contemporaries.

But what connection is there between Heywood's plays and later dramas. To say that Heywood was the "Father" of English comedy is misleading; for one finds no legitimate sons. John B. Moore, however, has suggested similarities between Heywood and the Elizabethans: "The future of the farce was not in the *Gammer Gurton* type, which had a very brief history. Farces began to be attached . . . as essential excrescences to the plots of serious plays. That is the place to search for the successors of *Johan Johan*, and the search is richly rewarded in plays of Greene, Peele, Lodge, Lyly, Shakespeare, Dekker, and Thomas Heywood."[9] But to be occasionally reminded of Heywood when reading these later writers is not to claim an influence.

Two plays from the middle of the century—*Thersites* (1537) and *Tom Tiler's Wife*—suggest the spirit of Heywood's farces and perhaps can be legitimately classified as a part of the Heywood legacy. A. W. Pollard has even suggested Heywood as a possible author of the anonymous *Thersites*.[10] The play, however, reflects Classical sources, although one passage may allude to the Pardoner's journey to Hell:

> If no man will with me battle take,
> A voyage to hell quickly I will make,
> And there I will beat the devil and his dame,
> And bring the souls away: I fully intend the same.
> After that in hell I have ruffled so,
> Straight to old Purgatory will I go.
> I will clean that, [and] so purge [it] round about,
> That we shall need no pardons to help them out.
>   (Dodsley, I, 402)

Heywood's *Johan Johan* may have influenced the anonymous *Tom Tiler*, not published until 1661, but probably written around 1553. John Farmer, recognizing obvious similarities, published the two plays under the title *Two Tudor Shrew Plays* (London, 1908). The main incident of the play is pure farce. Tom, the victim of a shrewish wife who alternates between beating her husband and gossiping with her cronies, laments his plight to a friend Tom Tayler. Tayler disguises himself as Tom Tiler and beats Strife until she vows always to honor and obey him. The next scene shows us Tom Tiler and Strife together; Strife is crying, begging him not to beat her again and asking why he has been so cruel. The perplexed Tom reveals that it was not he, but Tom Tayler, that had beaten her. The enraged Strife takes instant revenge upon her naïve husband. The farce is over, but Patience enters to reconcile the three main participants and the play ends with a song. *Tom Tiler* is one of the few English plays that manifest the simple structure of French farce.

Finally, Heywood's position in early Tudor drama is unique. He founded no tradition and noticeably influenced no successor. Three of his plays are medieval disputations that reflect the humanistic thought of the More circle. His three farces are lively, comical, realistic, and exhibit a keen dramatic sense; but they owe much to Chaucer and to contemporary French farce. As a dramatist, he is finally a man of his age who consciously looked backward and to his contemporaries, both in England and on the Continent. He dramatized current ideas; satirized obvious faults in the clergy; and turned, as his fellow dramatists did to a lesser extent, from abstractions to real persons. If Heywood did influence later writers, the effects are not discernible. Yet the reader can still enjoy three of his plays for their own intrinsic value. Such a statement is sufficient praise for a Tudor dramatist.

But Heywood's contemporaries and followers respected him as a mad, merry wit, not as a dramatist. A comic, a warm, humane satirist, Heywood entertained with witty turns of phrase and short merry tales. And, if we can judge from the number of editions of his works, his readers thoroughly enjoyed him. First published in 1562, Heywood's complete works were reprinted four times—1566, 1576, 1587, 1598—before the end of the century; and each generation in the latter part of the century had available a storehouse of English proverbs. In an age when the proverb was in high esteem, Heywood was recognized as an expert practitioner of this genre.[11] Heywood, furthermore, established a firm tradition in the English epigram. After his death, Heywood's fame depended upon his proverbs and witty *Epigrams*.[12] Francis Meres, John Heath (*Century of Epigrams*), and George Puttenham will afford sufficient support:

These and many other Epigrammatists the Latin tongue hath, Q. Catulus, Porcius Licinius, Quintus Cornificius, Martial, Cnoeus Getulicus, and wittie Sir Thomas Moore: so in English we have these Heywood, Drante, Kendal, Bastard, Dauies.[13]

> Heywood the old English epigrammatist
> Had wit at will, and art was all he mist:
> But now adaies we of the modern frie
> Have art and labour with wits penurie.[14]

. . . the Epigrammatist, who for the myrth and quicknesse of his conceits more then for any good learning was in him came to be well benefited by the king.[15]

It is too easy to make a false or overhasty judgment on Heywood. Some disparage his efforts, claiming that he too often worked in a tired tradition; others insist upon his originality and subtle influences upon later literature. His true importance lies somewhere between these extremes. He experimented, but he also continued in the traditional vein. His humor is occasionally coarse, but always broad and humane. He is a conservative, but is aware of the shortcomings of both secular and religious life and satirizes them with feeling but without venom. He reflects the age, the turmoil, the controversies of early sixteenth-century England, but he also transcends the mere topicalities, creating witty poems and concise interludes that can still be enjoyably read. After More and Erasmus, Tudor England offers no major literary figure; the next level is ruled by John Skelton and Thomas Heywood. It is not a lofty position on Mount Parnassus, but in its time was significant.

Notes and References

Chapter One

1. Quoted in *England Under the Early Tudors (1485-1529)*, C. H. Williams (New York, 1925), p. 64.
2. Christopher Morris, *The Tudors* (New York, 1956), p. 75.
3. Report by Giustinian, October 10, 1519. Quoted in *England Under the Early Tudors*, p. 89.
4. *Peacham's Compleat Gentleman*, introduction by G. S. Gordon (Oxford, 1906), p. 95. See also G. C. Moore-Smith, "John Heywood The Dramatist, A Freeman of London," *Notes and Queries*, X (1914), 128.
5. Anthony à Wood, *Athenae Oxonienses*, ed. Philip Bliss, I (London, 1813), 348.
6. Quotations from the non-dramatic works, except *The Spider and the Fly*, are from Burton A. Milligan, ed., *John Heywood's "Works" and Miscellaneous Short Poems* (Urbana, 1956). The epigrams will be hereafter noted thus: *The fyrste Hundred of Epigrammes*—I; *Three hundred Epigrammes upon three hundred prouerbes*—III; *The fifth hundred of Epigrams*—V; *A sixt hundred of Epigrammes*—VI. Thus the above epigram would be V, 55.
7. William Roper, *The Life of Sir Thomas More* in *Two Early Tudor Lives*, ed. Richard Sylvester and Davis P. Harding (New Haven, 1962), p. 254.
8. E. M. G. Routh, *Sir Thomas More and His Friends, 1477-1535* (London, 1934), p. 142.
9. *King's Book of Payments, Henry VIII, Exch., T. of R., Miscellaneous Books*, vol. 216, p. 201. The date is August 1. For earlier entry see *ibid.*, p. 94. I will not again trace all the various payments and gifts of land to Heywood from 1519-58 since such records shed little light on his writings. I have, however, listed many of these grants in the chronological table.

If the student is interested in a more detailed analysis, he should consult Robert Bolwell, *Life and Works of John Heywood* (New York, 1921); A. W. Reed, *Early Tudor Drama* (London, 1926), Chapter II, "The Heywoods"; Wilhelm Swoboda, *John Heywood als Dramatiker* (Wien, 1888); and for a controversial interpretation Charles W. Wallace, *The Evolution of the English Drama Up To Shakespeare*

(Berlin, 1912); also see R. de la Bere, *John Heywood: Entertainer* (London, 1937) and several articles listed in the bibliography, especially T. S. Graves, "The Heywood Circle and the Reformation," *Modern Philology*, X (1913), 533-72.

Editions of the original records are also available: J. S. Brewer *et al.*, *Letters and Papers of the Reign of Henry VIII* (London, 1862); Albert Feuillerat, *Documents Relating to the Office of the Revels in the Time of Queen Elizabeth* (Louvain, 1908); *Documents Relating to the Revels at Court in the Time of King Edward VI and Queen Mary* (Louvain, 1914).

10. J. Payne Collier, *The History of English Dramatic Poetry*, I (London, 1879), 73 and 77. For original entry see *Household Books of Henry VIII, 1509-1518*, Add. Mss. 21481, f. 177b.

11. Quoted in Routh, p. 20.

12. Pearl Hogrefe, *The Sir Thomas More Circle* (Urbana, 1959).

13. Giustinian, *Despatches*, ii, p. 314. Quoted in *England Under the Early Tudors*, p. 90.

14. *The Life and Death of Cardinal Wolsey* in *Two Early Tudor Lives*, ed. Richard S. Sylvester and Davis P. Harding (New Haven, 1962), p. 26.

15. R. de la Bere, *John Heywood: Entertainer* (London, 1937), p. 27.

16. John Bale, *Scriptorum Illustrium . . . Catalogus* (1557-58), II, 110; reprinted in Wallace, p. 79.

17. John Pitseus, *Relationum Historicarum de Rebus Anglicis Tomus Primus* (Paris, 1619), p. 753; reprinted in Bolwell, p. 168.

18. One point should be clarified. Both Wallace (p. 82) and Bolwell (p. 18) claim that Heywood was appointed steward in 1528; Reed (p. 42) argues that Heywood's period of court activity ended in 1528 and that he retired on a pension, returning to the active court life when Edward came to the throne; Reed would have Heywood's appointment as steward occur in 1552.

The problem is one of interpreting the entries. The entry for 1528 does not specifically mention a position; but, since the cancellation of the payment in 1558 refers to the two earlier sums—£10 in 1528 and £40 in 1552—Bolwell and Wallace have assumed that Henry VIII first made the appointment. That Heywood would retire from court while his friend More was becoming Chancellor does not seem likely. I think it safe to assume that Heywood was connected with the court throughout his adult life. Would Henry have pardoned Heywood in 1544 if he had retired from court circles some sixteen years prior? Neither interpretation, however, disturbs our concept of Heywood or aids our understanding of his works. The entry in question is recorded in *Exchequer of Receipt, Auditor's Warrant Books*, vol. 8, f. 138b.

19. J. S. Brewer *et al.*, *Letters and Papers of Henry VIII*, V, iii, pp. 445, 479.

20. A. W. Reed, *Early Tudor Drama* (London, 1926), p. 45.

21. Frederick Madden, *Privy Purse Expenses of the Princess Mary* (London, 1831), p. 62.

22. Charles W. Wallace, *The Evolution of the English Drama Up To Shakespeare* (Berlin, 1912), p. 84; E. K. Chambers, *The Medieval Stage*, II (Oxford, 1903), 203.

23. Robert W. Bolwell, *The Life and Works of John Heywood* (New York, 1921), p. 55.

24. Bolwell, pp. 30-31.

25. Brewer, *Letters and Papers of Henry VIII*, V, xiv, pt. ii, p. 340.

26. *Acts and Monuments*, ed. Stephen Reed Cattley, V (London, 1838), 528. The year of the recantation is 1544.

27. *Metamorphosis of Ajax;* quoted in Bolwell, p. 40. The identity of the gentleman of the chamber is not known.

28. Albert Feuillerat, ed., *Documents Relating to the Revels at Court in the Time of King Edward VI and Queen Mary* (Louvain, 1914), pp. xiv, 141, 142, 145.

29. *Ibid.*, p. 142.

30. John Stow, *Annales* (London, 1631), p. 617.

31. *Patent Rolls, 1 and 2 Philip and Mary*, pt. 8, m. 40; pt. 4, m. 16.

32. William Cambden, *Remains Concerning Britain*, ed. T. Moule (London, 1870), p. 314.

33. Robert Lemon, ed., *Calendar of State Papers, Domestic Series of the Reigns of Edward VI, Mary, Elizabeth, 1547-1580* (London, 1856), p. 112.

34. John Nichols, ed., *The Diary of Henry Machyn, 1550-1563* (London, 1848), p. 206.

35. Reed, p. 68.

36. Quoted in W. Bang, "Acta Anglo-Lovaniensia: John Heywood und sein Kreis," *Englische Studien*, XXXVIII (1907), 239.

37. Bang, p. 248.

38. Quoted in Bang, p. 235.

39. Mary Anne Everett Greene, ed., *Calendar of State Papers, Domestic Series, of the Reign of Elizabeth, 1566-1579* (London, 1871), document 1615, p. 581.

40. Bolwell, p. 68.

41. Quoted in A. W. Reed, p. 36.

42. *Ibid.*, pp. 35-36.

43. Quoted in Bang, p. 236.

44. *Ibid.*, p. 236.

45. *Ibid.*, p. 236.

46. *Ibid.*, p. 237.

47. The jest is preserved by Pitseus.

48. Bang, p. 250, has a genealogical table that demonstrates graphically the close relationship between the More family and the Rastell family.

1. Julian Sharman, ed. *The Proverbs of John Heywood* (London, 1874), p. xv. Burton Milligan has an excellent summary of the unfavorable criticism of Heywood's poetry in the nineteenth and twentieth centuries in his edition of Heywood.

2. Morris Palmer Tilley, *A Dictionary of the Proverbs in the Sixteenth and Seventeenth Centuries* (Michigan, 1950), p. vi.

3. Rudolph E. Habenicht, ed., *John Heywood's "A Dialogue of Proverbs"* (Los Angeles, 1963), p. 17.

4. Cf. Bartlett Jere Whiting, *Proverbs in the Earlier English Drama* (Cambridge, Mass., 1938), p. xi: "The popularity of homely sayings at the height of the Elizabethan period was no more than a continuation along familiar paths." Heywood himself, however, uses proverbs sparingly in his plays. Only Neither-lover-nor-loved and Johan Johan quote proverbs to any degree. Heywood's interest in proverbs, reflected in his *Dialogue of Proverbs* and the many epigrams upon proverbs, has no parallel in his dramas.

5. Habenicht, pp. 49-50.

6. Is it merely coincidence that More divided his two books of *Utopia* by having the participants retire for dinner?

7. The full title of the 1562 edition: "Iohn heywoodes / woorkes. / A dialogue conteynyng the / number of the effectuall prouerbes in / the Englishe tounge, compact in / a matter concernynge / two maner of ma- / ryages. / With one hundred of Epigrammes; and / three hundred of Epigrammes / upon three hundred pro- / verbes: and a fifth / hundred of E- / pigrams. / Whervnto are now newly added / a syxt hundred of Epigrams / by the sayde Iohn / Heywood. / Londini. / ANNO christi. / 1562."

8. Hoyt Hopewell Hudson, *The Epigram in the English Renaissance* (Princeton, 1947), p. 30. Hudson is primarily concerned with More and other Latin epigrammatists. An important point he makes about these writers suggests the atmosphere into which Heywood introduced his English epigrams: ". . . literary conventions demanded that a man of learning should produce epigrams, whether merely to display his wit or to pay a tribute to a new book, a noble patron, or a great man recently dead" (81).

9. Burton Milligan, "Humor and Satire in Heywood's Epigrams," *Studies in Honor of T. W. Baldwin,* ed. Don Cameron Allen (Urbana, 1958), p. 16. Milligan, p. 16, divides the humorous epigrams into the following categories: "epigrams dependent upon puns and other verbal quibbles; narrative epigrams treating ridiculous or extravagant situations like those of jestbooks and animal fables; and epigrams

whose humor arises from flitings, ingenious invective, and the exchange of witty insults." A meaningful classification of all six hundred epigrams is almost impossible, but in his edition, Milligan again offers a tentative division: "The six hundred epigrams of Heywood are of such varied types as epigrams based upon proverbs (the most numerous and best-known group); narrative epigrams, with episodes resembling the drolleries of the jest books; animal-fable epigrams; epigrams based upon the dramatization of elaborate puns; reflective epigrams on subjects as diverse as books and cheese; and wholly personal epigrams, in which Heywood frequently made himself the butt of the jest" (14).

10. Epigram 62 of the Sixth Hundred Epigrams ("Thankes to god and good people, Powles goth vp well: / Powles goth vp, but when goth poolyng downe: that tell.") refers to the building of St. Paul's after the fire of 1561. In several epigrams—V, 8; 63; 64; 65—Heywood satirized the debasement of the silver coins. See Milligan, *Works*, pp. 290-91.

11. Bolwell, pp. 135-36, recounts this incident, which is preserved by Ellis Heywood in *Il Moro*, by Cresacre More in *Life of Sir Thomas More*, and by Erasmus in *Apothegms*.

12. The page numbers are from John S. Farmer, ed., *The Spider and the Fly* (London, 1908). I have collated Farmer's edition with a microfilm copy of the 1556 edition, and the spelling is that of the original edition.

13. Bolwell, p. 144.

14. Quoted in Bolwell, p. 137.

15. David R. Hauser, "The Date of John Heywood's *The Spider and the Flie*," *Modern Language Notes*, LXX (1955), 17.

16. Hauser, p. 18.

17. Jakob Haber, *John Heywood's "The Spider and the Flie"* (Berlin, 1900), pp. 97-98.

18. Haber, pp. 78ff.

19. Bolwell, p. 143.

20. Quoted in R. J. Schoeck, "A Source for Heywood's *Spider and the Flie*," *Notes and Queries*, CXCVI (1951), 296.

21. Haber, pp. 111, 112.

Chaper Three

1. These are not the complete names of the plays; for convenience, I refer to them in abbreviated form. John Farmer has edited the writings of Heywood in three volumes: I, *The Dramatic Works of John Heywood* (London, 1905); II, *The Proverbs, Epigrams, and Miscellanies of John Heywood* (London, 1906); III, *The Writings of John Heywood* (London, 1908) [*Spider and the Fly* and *Gentleness and Nobility*]. Farmer's edition is, however, inadequate, and I have chosen to use more accurate and more accessible texts.

Witty and Witless or *Witty* was not published during Heywood's life, but was preserved in manuscript. My text is Rupert de la Bere, *John Heywood: Entertainer* (London, 1937). *Love* is *The Play of Love* printed in 1533 by William Rastell. John Waley reprinted the play between 1546 and 1586. My text is Alois Brandl (who printed Waley's edition), *Quellen Des Weltlichen Dramas In England* (Strassburg, 1898). *Weather* is *The Play of the Wether*, printed in 1533 by William Rastell. The text is J. Q. Adams, *Chief Pre-Shakespearean Dramas* (Cambridge, 1924). *The Four PP* is *The Play Called the Four PP*, printed between 1543 and 1547 by William Middleton. My text is Adams. *The Pardoner and the Friar* was printed by William Rastell in 1533. My text is de la Bere. *Johan Johan* is *A Mery Play Betwene Johan Johan, the Husbande, Tyb, His Wyfe, and Syr Johan, the Preest*, printed by William Rastell in 1533. My text is Adams. The references for all quotations from Heywood's plays will be thus limited to line or page numbers and will be included in the text.

2. K. W. Cameron, *Authorship and Sources of "Gentleness and Nobility": A Study in Early Tudor Drama* (Raleigh, North Carolina, 1941); C. W. Wallace, p. 1.

3. Wallace, p. 50.

4. *Ibid.*, p. 51.

5. *Ibid.*, p. 52.

6. Reed, p. 125.

7. The date of *Johan Johan* is disputed. Most critics interpret the date (February 12, 1533) to mean 1534 (Chambers, II, 445), but Reed (p. 81) argues for 1533.

8. K. W. Cameron, *The Background of John Heywood's "Witty and Witless"* (Raleigh, North Carolina, 1941), offers the only book-length study of the play. Cameron sees it as a part of the More humanistic circle: "Heywood's play springs immediately from the atmosphere of Erasmus and More, and is opposed to the opinions expressed in the many works of which the French *Dyalogue* is representative. The humanists attempted to vindicate man's reason and attacked unbelief, fatalism, and morbid fears. I, therefore, see in the conclusion of *Witty and Witless* an unusually fine specimen of English humanistic thought at its best" (14).

9. In the French debate there is no source for Jerome; only two characters participate in the dispute and the fool, who advocates God's way, is allowed to win. I do not think that Heywood borrowed much, if anything, from the French play. I discuss the sources in the next chapter. See also Karl Young, "The Influence of French Farce Upon the Plays of John Heywood," *Modern Philology*, II (1904), 109ff.; Cameron, *Background of . . . "Witty"*; and Ian Maxwell, *French Farce and John Heywood* (Melbourne, 1946).

10. Desiderus Erasmus, *The Praise of Folly*, trans. Hoyt Hopewell Hudson (Princeton, 1941), p. 50.

11. Robert Withington, "Paronomasia in John Heywood's Plays," *Smith College Studies in Modern Languages*, XXI (1939-40), 234, argues that this distinction between pleasure and content gives the play a "philosophical interest"; the discussion is obviously a digression, but I would insist that it also has dramatic relevancy.

12. J. E. Bernard, Jr., *The Prosody of the Tudor Interlude* (New Haven, 1939), pp. 63-66. Bernard has a summary table of the verse patterns for each play.

13. Harold Newcomb Hillebrand, "On the Authorship of the Interludes Attributed to John Heywood," *Modern Philology*, XIII (1915), 270.

14. Jupiter is turning to his subjects to help him solve a dispute raging in heaven between Saturn (cold), Phebus (heat), Eolus (wind), and Phebe (rain). These gods have surrendered their powers to Jupiter who is requesting aid from the former victims of the dispute: ". . . we hyther are dyscendyd / . . . [to] satysfye and content / All maner people whyche have ben offendyd / By any wether mete to be amendyd:" (86-89). David Bevington comments upon Jupiter's first scene: "The situation lends itself to comic bombast, and Jupiter exploits it. The audience would see a gentle parody of kingship in a familiar tradition of court entertainment." "Is John Heywood's *Play of the Weather* Really about the Weather?" *Renaissance Drama*, VII (1964), 13.

15. This speech should be compared to a theme of *Gentleness and Nobility*, a contemporary play probably by John Rastell. The play is a debate between a knight, a merchant, and a plowman over the qualities of a gentleman. The knight, as does the Gentleman in the speech above, claims a special prerogative from birth. Similar philosophy does not indicate common authorship, but does reflect a common topic of the period—the qualities of the gentleman, a subject which is handled by the sundry courtesy literature of the century. I discuss in detail *Gentleness and Nobility* in Chapter 5.

16. A ranger was a keeper of a forest.

17. The only book-length study of the play is K. W. Cameron, *John Heywood's "Play of the Wether"* (Raleigh, North Carolina, 1941). This is a thorough, scholarly investigation of the sources, background, and themes of the play. He concludes: "*Wether* is first of all a compliment to Henry VIII, a strong argument for Henry's complete control of the government, and a plea for social solidarity under his direction on the part of the entire nation" (p. 56). David Bevington, "Is John Heywood's *Play of the Weather* Really about the Weather?" comments: "Heywood's ultimate view of political life, then, is that the parts of society can never understand the whole. Only the king can act as umpire between elements seeking continu-

ally to destroy one another. To do so he must have knowledge of the claims of each estate and so listens to partial arguments without accepting the advice of any one counselor" (18).

18. Line 1027 of *Weather;* the boy says that Jupiter has come "This nyght to suppe here wyth my lorde."

19. Pearl Hogrefe, *The Sir Thomas More Circle* (Urbana, 1959), p. 309.

20. James M. Osborn, ed., *The Autobiography of Thomas Whythorne* (Oxford, 1961), pp. 13-14.

21. *Ibid.,* p. 74.

22. *Ibid.,* p. 74.

23. *Ibid.,* pp. 72-73.

24. See especially Wesley Phy, "Chronology of John Heywood's Plays," *Englische Studien,* LXXIV (1940), 27-41.

25. A palmer traveled from religious shrine to religious shrine, and our palmer's list is quite impressive. Any who have read Chaucer know that a pardoner was licensed to sell papal pardons and indulgences; Heywood's pardoner is obviously borrowed from Chaucer. The pothecary wandered over the country selling various herbs and potions as medicines. The two shared a common bond of corruption.

26. John Walker McCain, "Heywood's *The Foure PP;* A Debt to Skelton," *Notes and Queries* CLXXIV (1938), 205, suggests that Heywood borrowed the name of the woman and the incident from a passage in Skelton's "Colin Clout."

27. See George Lyman Kittredge, "John Heywood and Chaucer," *American Journal of Philology,* IX (1888), 473-74. Quotations from Chaucer are from *The Complete Works of Geoffrey Chaucer,* F. N. Robinson, ed. (Boston, 1933).

28. Hillebrand, p. 278; Reed, pp. 141-44; Bernard, p. 43; Bolwell, p. 111.

29. Reed, p. 141.

30. A. W. Pollard, "John Heywood: Critical Essay," in *Representative English Comedies,* ed. Charles Mills Gayley (London, 1907), p. 40.

31. Sidney Thomas, "Wolsey and French Farces," *London Times Literary Supplement,* Dec., 7, 1935, p. 838.

32. Phy, p. 27.

33. The counterparts of the burlesqued sermon are the French *Sermon Joyeux.* There is a French farce, *Sermon Joyeux de Bien Boyre* which has two actors, a preacher and a cook; the latter's constant interruptions and questions burlesque the cleric's sermon and turn what at one level might be serious into comedy. The same is true in our play. If we took the Friar's lines out of context and ignored his hypocrisy we would have a plausible sermon. But when we are subjected to the Pardoner at the same time, the result can only be humorous. David Lyndesay's *Ane Satyre of the Thrie Estaits*

also contains a burlesqued sermon when Folly delivers a sermon, lines 4466ff.

34. The assignment of the speeches in this episode has been disputed because of obvious errors in Rastell's text. See Stanley Sultan, "The Audience Participation Episode in *Johan Johan*," *JEGP*, LII (1953), 491-97. Who speaks these lines has no effect upon the main point—the audience is a participator, not merely an observer. Adams gives the entire speech to Johan Johan (242-59). Pollard assigns the following lines to Tyb: 241-44; 246-57; 260-63. Sultan's division is as follows: Tyb: 241; 252-57; 260-63; Johan Johan: 242-51; 258-59; 264. The audience-participation scene occurs in the French play that Heywood was translating; since Sultan does not mention the influence of the source, I reproduce this exchange. It offers another example of Heywood's handling of his source, a problem I discuss in the next chapter. We should note that Sultan's division of the episode is not supported by the exchange in the French play. Professor Cohen has divided the text similarly, but in the original the entire passage is given to the man.

L'HOMME:
Actendez, je desuies ma robe,
J'ay si grant paour qu'on la me robe
Que je ne scay où la bouter.
Qui se vente de la garder?
Ha! elle sera icy bien,
Hé! velà ung pi[s]sat de chien,
Elle seroit toute gastée.
Je la misse en la cheminée,
Mais on la bruleroit aux boutz.

LA FEMME:
Sire, mettez-la dessoubz vous
Ou entre vous et la boutte,
Mais venez cà!

L'HOMME:
Gardez-la, je la vous aporte.

LA FEMME:
Hé! il est auprès de la porte,
Bien s'en pourroit fouir atout.
Je la mectray icy à ce bout
Et qu'âme ne marche dessus,
Ostez la torche de dessus.

L'HOMME:
Veez me cy près d'aller or sus,
Ne dictes pas qu'à moy il tienne. (252-71)

Farce du Paste in *Recueil De Farces Francaises Inedites Du XV Siecle,* ed. Gustave Cohen (Cambridge, Mass., 1949).

35. David Bevington, *From "Mankind" to Marlowe* (Cambridge, Mass., 1962), pp. 38-42.

36. Chambers, II, p. 184.

Chapter Four

1. The traditional view of Heywood is best expressed by Wilhelm Swoboda, *John Heywood als Dramatiker* (Wien, 1888), who sees Heywood as an integral part of the developing dramatic tradition: "Die komischen *Interludes* John Heywoods sind legitime Nachkommen der Moralitaten und werden mit Recht als das Bindegleid zwischen diesen allegorisch-didaktischen Spielen und dem regularem englischen Lustspiel angesehen" (55). (The comic interludes of John Heywood are legitimate successors of the moralities and are regarded correctly as the connecting link between the allegorical, didactic plays and the regular English comedy.)

2. A. W. Pollard, "John Heywood: Critical Essay," p. 5.

3. Ian Maxwell, p. 95. The French play has been edited by L. J. N. Monmerque, *Melanges de la Société des bibliophiles francais,* VI (Paris, 1829).

4. Bolwell, p. 88.

5. F. Holthausen, "Zu John Heywoods *Wetterspiel,*" *Archiv,* CXVI (1906), 103-4. J. Q. Adams, "John Heywood's *Play of the Weather,*" *Modern Language Notes,* XXII (1907), 262. K. W. Cameron, John Heywood's *"Play of the Weather,"* pp. 20-22.

6. Pearl Hogrefe, *The Sir Thomas More Circle,* p. 297. *"The Four PP's* . . . uses the imaginative fantasy of a trip to the underworld, with the details and spirit of Lucian's Menippus." I find this statement too vague to actually be helpful. The details in Lucian are not repeated in Heywood's tale and the purpose of the two satires is entirely different.

7. Ian Maxwell, pp. 73ff.

8. *Ibid.,* pp. 83, 84.

9. See Karl Young, pp. 101-5; also Ian Maxwell, who lists similar details in *Pernet* and *Johan Johan,* pp. 61-65. In an article that appeared four years after Craik had demonstrated that Heywood's play was a translation of another farce, Stanley Sultan argued for Heywood's originality in transforming the French farce, *Pernet;* see *"Johan Johan* and Its Debt to French Farce," *Journal of English and Germanic Philology,* LIII (1954), 23-27.

10. T. W. Craik, "The True Source of John Heywood's *Johan Johan,*" *Modern Language Review,* XLV (1950), 289-95. My quotations are from G. Cohen's edition of the play.

11. Craik, pp. 293-94.

Chapter Five

1. I have used the following editions for the quotations from the several plays referred to in this chapter. In the text I will therefore offer only page or line numbers. *Gentleness and Nobility*, the microfilm copy of the first edition, but I cite page numbers from John S. Farmer, ed., *The Dramatic Works* (London, 1908). *Fulgens and Lucrece*, ed. F. S. Boas and A. W. Reed (Oxford 1926). *Calisto and Melibaea, Dodsley's Old English Plays*, ed. W. Carew Hazlitt (London, 1874), vol. I. *Nature of the Four Elements, Dodsley*, vol. I. *Wit and Science*, J. Q. Adams, ed., *Chief Pre-Shakespearean Dramas*. *Nature*, Brandl. *Magnificence, The Complete Poems of John Skelton*, ed. Philip Henderson (London, 1948). *King John*, J. M. Manly, ed., *Specimens of the Pre-Shakesperean Drama* (Boston, 1897), vol. I.

2. Bolwell, pp. 90-95; C. F. Tucker-Brooke, "*Gentleness and Nobility*; the Authorship and Source," *Modern Language Review*, VI (1911), 458-61; K. W. Cameron, *Authorship and Sources of "Gentleness and Nobility"* (Raleigh, North Carolina, 1941), p. 88.

3. Wallace, p. 52. Frederick Boas, *Tudor Drama* (Oxford, 1933), pp. 7-9; A. W. Reed, p. 116; Esther Dunn, "John Rastell and *Gentleness and Nobility*," *MLR*, XII (1917), 278.

4. Reed, p. 119.

5. C. F. Tucker-Brooke, "*Gentleness and Nobility*; the Authorship and Source," pp. 458-61. Tucker-Brooke lists parallel passages and argues that the initial idea for the entire plot stems from Chaucer's tale. I think that he tends to overstate his case, but there are definitely slight verbal parallels, not, however, to the extent of *The Pardoner and the Friar* and Chaucer's Pardoner.

6. Bernard, p. 53.

7. Albert Feuillerat, ed., *Documents Relating to the Revels at Court in the Time of King Edward VI and Queen Mary* (Louvain, 1914), assigns the play to Sir Thomas Chaloner (pp. 60, 278). Wallace, as I mentioned above, advances Cornish.

8. Cameron, *Background of "Witty and Witless*," pp. 60-61.

9. John B. Moore, *The Comic and the Realistic in English Drama* (Chicago, 1925), pp. 105-6.

10. Pollard, pp. 13-14.

11. I do not feel it is necessary to cite the many sixteenth- and seventeenth-century references to Heywood; these have been adequately collected in several places: Burton Milligan, ed., *Heywood's Works*, pp. 2-13; Bolwell, pp. 75-79; T. S. Graves, "On the Reputation of John Heywood," *Modern Philology*, XXI (1923), 209-13. Graves concludes his article with the following statement:

> A study of the allusions above together with those utilized by Bolwell reveals the fact that, whereas the men of the late sixteenth and early seventeenth centuries were not interested

> in Heywood as a dramatist, he was, in spite of his staunch
> Catholicism, held in high esteem by his immediate succes-
> sors as a wit, stylist, compiler of proverbs, and epigramma-
> tist. As such his real significance on Elizabethan literature
> is not brought out by a mere collection of the allusions to
> him; for it can be demonstrated, I think, that his non-
> dramatic works were rather freely utilized by writers of
> drama and satire who do not refer to him by name. (213)

Of course the euphuistic style embodies many proverbs, for which
Heywood may be in some way responsible. John W. Hales ("The
Date of "The First English Comedy,'" *Englische Studien*, XVIII
[1893], 408-21) attempts to prove the dependence of *Ralph Roister
Doister* on Heywood's *Dialogue of Proverbs*. He cites identical
phrases and allusions. Ewald Flugel ("Nicholas Udall: Critical
Essay" in *Representative English Comedies*, ed. Charles M. Gayley
[New York, 1903], p. 96) takes issue with Hales' theory. It is, of
course, difficult to use proverbs, which are a part of the colloquial
language, to prove an influence. We must be content to note
emphatically the popularity of Heywood's works during Elizabeth's
reign. His influence is too subtle to delineate more accurately.

12. Bolwell, p. 75.

13. Francis Meres, *Palladis Tamia* in *Elizabethan Critical Essays*,
ed. G. Gregory Smith (Oxford, 1904), II, 321.

14. Quoted in Bolwell, p. 78.

15. George Puttenham, *The Arte of English Poesie* in *Elizabethan
Critical Essays*, II, 63.

Selected Bibliography

PRIMARY SOURCES

ADAMS, JOHN QUINCY, ed. *Chief Pre-Shakespearean Dramas.* Cambridge: Houghton Mifflin, 1924. Excellent texts of *Weather, The Four PP,* and *Johan Johan.*

BOAS, FREDERICK, ed. *Five Pre-Shakespearean Dramas.* London: Oxford University Press, 1934. Text of *The Four PP.*

BRANDL, ALOIS. *Quellen des Weltlichen Dramas In England vor Shakespeare.* Strassburg: Karl J. Trübner, 1898. Brief, but informative discussion of the plays and a text of *Love, Weather,* and *Johan Johan.*

CAMERON, KENNETH WALTER. *Authorship and Sources of "Gentleness and Nobility": A Study in Early Tudor Drama.* Raleigh, North Carolina: The Thistle Press, 1941. Impressive gathering of contemporary ideas and analogues; Cameron argues for Heywood's authorship of the play and also edits *Gentleness.*

DE LA BERE, RUPERT. *John Heywood: Entertainer.* London: Allen and Unwin, 1937. Balanced, conservative analysis of Heywood's life and writings; bibliography; texts of *Witty, The Four PP, The Pardoner and the Friar,* and *Johan Johan.*

FAIRHOLT, F. W., ed. *A Dialogue on Wit and Folly.* London: Percy Society, vol. 20, 1846. Earliest edition of *Witty.* Fairholt's introduction is mainly a collection of quotations from the play and a summary of the plot.

FARMER, JOHN S., ed. *The Pardoner and the Friar, the Curate and Neigbour Pratt; The Foure PP.* London: Early English Drama Society, 1906. Convenient but weak text of the two farces.

———., ed. *The Works of John Heywood.* 3 vols. London: Early English Drama Society, 1905-8. Only complete edition of all of Heywood's works, including *Gentleness and Nobility.* The text is, however, inadequate; and a new edition of the plays is needed. For the titles of the separate volumes see Chapter Four, Note 1. No introduction, but word lists at the back of each volume.

———., ed. *Two Tudor Shrew Plays.* London: Early English Drama Society, 1908. Text of *Johan Johan.*

HABENICHT, RUDOLPH E., ed. *John Heywood's "A Dialogue of Proverbs."* Berkeley, California: University of California Press,

1963. An excellent edition and invaluable introduction, in which Dr. Habenicht discusses various marriage treatises of the period. There are also indexes to the proverbs.

HAZLITT, W. CAREW, ed. *Dodsley's Old English Plays*. Vol. I. London: Reeves, 1874. Texts of *The Pardoner and the Friar* and *The Four PP.*

HEYWOOD, JOHN. *The Proverbs and Epigrams of John Heywood*. London: The Spenser Society, Issue no. 1, 1867. A poor edition; no introduction.

MANLY, JOHN MATTHEWS, ed. *Specimens of the Pre-Shaksperean Drama*. 2 vols. New York: Ginn & Co., 1897. Text of *The Four PP.*

MILLIGAN, BURTON A., ed. *John Heywood's "Works" and Miscellaneous Short Poems*. Urbana, Illinois: University of Illinois Press, 1956. A scholarly edition and an excellent introduction, in which Dr. Milligan traces the reputation of Heywood. An indispensable edition for the student of Heywood.

POLLARD, ALFRED W. "John Heywood: Critical Essay." *Representative English Comedies*. Ed. Charles Mills Gayley. London: Macmillan, 1907. Suggests Heywood as the author of *Thersites,* but also offers a solid analysis of Heywood's value and influence. Text of *Weather* and *Johan Johan.*

SCOTT, W. *Ancient British Drama*. Vol. I. London: Miller, 1810. Text of *The Four PP.*

SHARMAN, JULIAN, ed. *The Proverbs of John Heywood*. London: George Bell and Sons, 1874. An early edition; introduction dismisses the poem as a curiosity piece, but does discuss the plays. Adversely critical of Heywood.

WARD, A. W. Introduction. *The Spider and the Flie*. London: Spenser Society, 1894. In a perceptive introduction, Ward discusses the poem as a reflection of social discontent.

SECONDARY SOURCES

ADAMS, JOHN QUINCY. "John Heywood's *The Play of the Weather,*" *Modern Language Notes*, XXII (1907), 262. Points to a passage in Lucian's *Icaromenippus* which may have suggested the outline of *Weather.*

BANG, W. "Acta Anglo-Lovaniensia: John Heywood und sein kreis," *Englische Studien*, XXXVIII (1907), 234-50. Deals with the period of Heywood's voluntary exile; quotes from the contemporary documents.

BERDAN, JOHN M. *Early Tudor Poetry*. New York: Macmillan, 1920. Good discussion of *The Spider and the Fly.*

BERNARD, J. E. *Prosody of the Tudor Interlude*. New Haven: Yale University Press, 1939. Metrical analysis of Heywood's plays;

notes the similarities between *Gentleness* and other plays in the canon.

BEVINGTON, DAVID. *From "Mankind" to Marlowe*. Cambridge, Mass.: Harvard University Press, 1962. Thorough study of the tradition of doubling and the structure of sixteenth-century drama. Develops criteria for court and popular drama.

—————. "Is John Heywood's *Play of the Weather* Really About the Weather?" *Renaissance Drama*, VII (1964), 11-19. Bevington interprets the play as a historical allegory.

BOAS, FREDERICK. *Tudor Drama*. Oxford: The Clarendon Press, 1933. Survey of the drama of the period; briefly discusses Heywood's plays.

BOAS, FREDERICK S., and A. W. REED, eds. *Fulgens and Lucrece*. Oxford: Oxford University Press, 1926. Text of the play and brief critical and historical introduction.

BOLWELL, ROBERT W. *The Life and Works of John Heywood*. New York: Columbia University Press, 1921. Good, full-length treatment of life and all the works. Also includes a bibliography and appendices which reprint Rastell's will, Heywood's recantation, Pitseus' brief biographical sketch, and a list of revels at the court of Henry VIII.

BREWER, J. S., ed. *Letters and Papers of the Reign of Henry VIII*. London: G. E. Eyre, 1862. References to John Heywood.

BROOKE, C. F. TUCKER. "*Gentleness and Nobility*; the Authorship and Source," *Modern Language Review*, VI (1911), 458-61. Argues that Heywood is the author of *Gentleness*; points out borrowings from Chaucer.

—————. *The Tudor Drama*. New York: Houghton Mifflin, 1911. Important study of sixteenth-century drama; brief section on Heywood.

CAMBDEN, WILLIAM. *Remains Concerning Britain*. Ed. T. Moule. London: J. R. Smith, 1870. Cambden preserves a few of Heywood's witty sayings.

CAMERON, KENNETH WALTER. *The Background of John Heywood's "Witty and Witless."* Raleigh, North Carolina: Thistle Press, 1941. Thorough study of the sources and analogues of *Witty*; also includes a bibliography.

—————. *John Heywood's "Play of the Wether."* Raleigh, North Carolina: Thistle Press, 1941. Argues at length for *Icaromenippus* as the source; sees the play as a representative of that literature that deals with the conflict of social classes.

CHAMBERS, E. K. *The Medieval Stage*. 2 vols. Oxford: Clarendon Press, 1903. Indispensable for understanding the Tudor interlude.

COHEN, GUSTAVE, ed. *Recueil de Farces Francaises Inedites du XV Siècle*. Cambridge, Mass.: Mediaeval Academy of America,

1949. Contains the French farce that Heywood translated for *Johan Johan.*

COLLIER, J. PAYNE. *The History of English Dramatic Poetry and Annals of the Stage.* 3 vols. London: J. Murray, 1879. The first to claim that Heywood entered court service as early as 1514-15.

CRAIK, T. W. "Experiment and Variety in John Heywood's Plays," *Renaissance Drama,* VII (1964), 6-11. Essay uses three plays—*Weather, The Four PP, The Pardoner and the Friar*—to demonstrate Heywood's experiments and improvisations; too impressionistic.

————. "The True Source of John Heywood's *Johan Johan,*" *Modern Language Review,* XLV (1950), 289-95. Indispensable article; points out that Heywood's play is a close translation of a French farce.

————. *The Tudor Interlude.* Leicester: Leicester University Press, 1958. Excellent introduction to the staging of Heywood and his contemporaries.

DUNN, ESTHER C. "John Rastell and *Gentleness and Nobility,*" *Modern Language Review,* XII (1917), 266-78. Argues for John Rastell's authorship; article answers Brooke's argument.

FEUILLERAT, ALBERT, ed. *Documents Relating to the Revels at Court in the Time of King Edward VI and Queen Mary.* Louvain: Uystpruyst, 1914. Records and comments upon various dramatic activities of Heywood and others.

FOXE, JOHN. *Acts and Monuments.* Ed. Stephen Reed Cattley. Vol. V. London: R. B. Seeley, 1838. Preserves Heywood's recantation; discusses his part in the plot against Cranmer.

GRAVES, T. S. "On the Reputation of John Heywood," *Modern Philology,* XXI (1923), 209-13. Brings together various sixteenth- and seventeenth-century references to Heywood that Bolwell had not included.

————. "The Heywood Circle and the Reformation," *Modern Philology,* X (1913), 533-72. Attempts to support the idea that Heywood spent his youth at North Mimms in Hertfordshire and was early admitted to the More circle.

GREG, W. W. "Notes on Some Early Plays," *Library* (Series 4), XI (1931), 44-56. Discusses bibliographical problems of the later editions of *Weather.*

————. "An Unknown Edition of Heywood's *Play of Love,*" *Archiv,* CVI (1901), 141-43. A bibliographical problem.

HABER, JAKOB. *John Heywood's "The Spider and the Flie."* Berlin: E. Felber, 1900. Only book-length study of the poem; thorough and scholarly; poem is related to both historical events and other literature of the period.

HALES, JOHN W. "The Date of 'The First English Comedy,'" *Englische Studien,* XVIII (1893), 408-21. Points out similarities between Udall's *Ralph Roister Doister* and Heywood's *Dialogue of Proverbs* and suggests an influence.

HAUSER, DAVID R. "The Date of John Heywood's *The Spider and the Flie*," *Modern Language Notes*, LXX (1955), 15-18. Argues for a later dating of the poem—around 1555.

HILLEBRAND, HAROLD NEWCOMB. "On the Authorship of the Interludes Attributed to John Heywood," *Modern Philology*, XIII (1915), 267-80. Answers Wallace's argument that Cornish, not Heywood, wrote the plays. Hillebrand claims that Heywood is the author of the plays normally assigned to him, but does not enter the discussion about *Gentleness*.

HOGREFE, PEARL. *The Sir Thomas More Circle: A Program of Ideas and Their Impact on Secular Drama.* Urbana: University of Illinois Press, 1959. An excellent survey of the ideas of More and his circle on education, religious reform, government, and the bases of nobility and an analysis of the effect of these ideas on the contemporary drama. All of Heywood's plays are discussed.

HOLTHAUSEN, F. "Zu John Heywoods 'Wetterspiel,'" *Archiv*, CXVI (1906), 103-4. Points out the passage in Lucian's *Icaromenippus* which may have been Heywood's source. See Adams.

HUDSON, HOYT HOPEWELL. *The Epigram in the English Renaissance.* Princeton, New Jersey: Princeton University Press, 1947. Does not mention Heywood, but offers an important analysis of the sixteenth-century Latin epigram.

"J. H. The Father of English Comedy," *Times Literary Supplement*, August 24, 1922, p. 543. A review of Bolwell's book, but actually a brief biography and appreciation of Heywood.

KITTREDGE, GEORGE LYMAN. "John Heywood and Chaucer," *American Journal of Philology*, IX (1888), 473-74. Points out parallel passages in Heywood and Chaucer.

LEE, SIDNEY. *The French Renaissance in England.* New York: Scribner's, 1910. Essential book in understanding the influence of French culture on England in the early sixteenth century. Lee contends that Greene was influenced by Heywood.

LEMON, ROBERT, ed. *Calendar of State Papers, Domestic Series, of the Reigns of Edward VI, Mary, Elizabeth, 1547-1580.* London: Public Record Office, 1856. References to Heywood.

LONG, RICHARD. "John Heywood, Chaucer, and Lydgate," *Modern Language Notes*, LXIV (1949), 55-56. Suggests that Heywood's choice of protagonists in *The Pardoner and the Friar* was prompted by Lydgate's remark in referring to *The Canterbury Tales*: "he speaks of the Pardoner's 'Tellyng a tale to angre with the frere.'"

MAXWELL, IAN. *French Farce and John Heywood.* Melbourne: University of Melbourne Press, 1946. Excellent, thorough study of the plays; Maxwell argues that all of the plays have general affinities with French farce. One limitation is his discussion of the source—*Pernet*—of *Johan Johan*.

McCain, John Walker. "Heywood's *The Foure PP*: A Debt to Skelton," *Notes and Queries*, CLXXIV (1938), 205. Suggests Heywood got the idea for the Pardoner's visit to Hell and the woman's name from Skelton's "Colin Clout."

————. "Oratory, Rhetoric and Logic in the Writings of John Heywood," *Quarterly Journal of Speech*, XXVI (1940), 44-47. Stresses the influence of oratorical training on Heywood's writings and career.

Miller, Edwin Shepard. "Guilt and Penalty in Heywood's Pardoner's Lie," *Modern Language Quarterly*, X (1949), 58-60. Sees the lie as "an ultimate in misogyny."

Milligan, Burton A. "Humor and Satire in Heywood's Epigrams," *Studies in Honor of T. W. Baldwin*. Ed. Don Cameron Allen. Urbana: University of Illinois Press, 1958. pp. 16-33. Analyzes the types of humor in the epigrams and suggests some helpful categories.

Moore, John B. *The Comic and the Realistic in English Drama*. Chicago: University of Chicago Press, 1925. Interesting study of realistic comedy in the century, but Moore suggests an influence for Heywood that few critics would accept.

Moore-Smith, G. C. "John Heywood The Dramatist, A Freeman of London," *Notes and Queries*, Eleventh Series, X (1914), 128. Reprints some documents that connect a John Heywood with London; suggests that, if this Heywood is the dramatist, he may not have been born in London.

Morris, Christopher. *The Tudors*. New York: Macmillan, 1956. Well-written collection of essays on the Tudor monarchs.

Nichols, John Gough, ed. *The Diary of Henry Machyn, 1550-1563*. London: Cambden Society, 1848. Refers to Heywood's performance before Queen Elizabeth in 1559.

Osborn, James M., ed. *The Autobiography of Thomas Whythorne*. Oxford: Clarendon Press, 1961. Whythorne quotes fourteen lines from a lost Heywood play, "The Parts of Man."

Phy, Wesley. "Chronology of John Heywood's Plays," *Englische Studien*, LXXIV (1940), 27-41. Suggests a dramatic development in the Heywood canon; an excellent article.

Pitseus, John. *Relationum Historicarum de Rebus Anglicis Tomus Primus*. Paris: N.P., 1619. Contains a brief biographical sketch of Heywood.

Rathborne, Isabel E. "Another Interpretation of *Muiopotmos*," *Publications of the Modern Language Association*, XLIX (1934), 1050-68. Model for Spenser's poem was Heywoods epic.

REED, A. W. *Early Tudor Drama*. London: Methuen, 1926. Essential for understanding the life of Heywood and his connection with the More circle. Chapters on John Rastell and William Rastell are included.

ROUTH, E. M. G. *Sir Thomas More and His Friends, 1477-1535*. London: Oxford University Press, 1934. The point of view enables the reader to get a good glimpse of the intellectual atmosphere to which Heywood was early introduced.

SCHOECK, R. J. "A Common Tudor Expletive and Legal Parody in Heywood's *Play of Love*," *Notes and Queries*, CCI (1956), 375-76. Suggests that *torde*, meaning excrement, is a play on *tort*, the breach of duty.

————. "Satire of Wolsey in Heywood's *Play of Love*." *Notes and Queries*, CXCVI (1951), 112-14. Sees references in the play to a feud between Wolsey and the common lawyers.

————. "A Source for Heywood's *Spider and the Flie*," *Notes and Queries*, CXCVI (1951), 296-97. Suggests a passage from Erasmus, Chapter 6 of *The Education of a Christian Prince*, as a source.

STROINSKA, JOANNA. "John Heywood, 1494-1565," *Notes and Queries*, CLXXXIX (1945), 156-61. List of words occurring in Heywood's works that are listed in *OED* at a later date.

SULTAN, STANLEY. "The Audience-Participation Episode in *Johan Johan*," *Journal of English and Germanic Philology*, LII (1953), 491-97. Cogent argument for emending the incident where Johan Johan looks for someone to hold his coat.

————. "*Johan Johan* and Its Debt to French Farce," *Journal of English and Germanic Philology*, LIII (1954), 23-37. Argues for originality of Heywood in transforming the French farce, *Pernet;* but Craik had earlier proved that *Pernet* was not the source.

SWOBODA, WILHELM. *John Heywood als Dramatiker*. Vienna: Weiner Beiträge zur deutschen und englischen Philologie, 1888. Important early book on Heywood; besides the biographical and critical sections, Swoboda offers a lengthy study of versification and an analysis of his supposed influence on later drama.

SYLVESTER, RICHARD S., and P. HARDING DAVIS, eds. *Two Early Tudor Lives*. New Haven, Connecticut: Yale University Press, 1962. Texts of two important biographies: *Life and Death of Cardinal Wolsey* by George Cavendish; *Life of Sir Thomas More* by William Roper. Book also contains a short, informative introduction.

TANNENBAUM, SAMUEL A., and DOROTHY R. *John Heywood: A Concise Bibliography*. New York: S. A. Tannenbaum, 1946. Valuable bibliography.

THOMAS, SIDNEY. "Wolsey and French Farces," *Times Literary Supplement*, Dec. 7, 1935, p. 838. Reprints a letter that reveals the French influence on Wolsey and court drama.

TILLEY, MORRIS PALMER, ed. *A Dictionary of the Proverbs in the Sixteenth and Seventeenth Centuries*. Michigan: University of Michigan Press, 1950. Valuable research tool; helpful introduction.

WALLACE, CHARLES WILLIAM. *The Evolution of the English Drama up to Shakespeare*. Berlin: G. Reimer, 1912. Suggests that William Cornish wrote several of the plays traditionally assigned to Heywood.

WARTON, THOMAS. *The History of English Poetry from the Eleventh to the Seventeenth Century*. London: Ward, Lock, & Co., 1870. Harsh, critical analysis of Heywood; an antidote to some of the more lavish praise.

WHITING, BARTLETT J. *Proverbs in the Earlier English Drama*. Cambridge, Mass.: Harvard University Press, 1938. Study of the frequency of the use of proverbs in early drama. Heywood uses them seldom in his plays.

WILLIAM, C. H. *England Under the Early Tudors*. London: Longmans, 1925. Selections of original documents of the period from 1485 to 1529 illustrate the political, ecclesiastical, and social conditions.

WITHINGTON, ROBERT. "Paronomasia in John Heywood's Plays," *Smith College Studies in Modern Languages*, XXI (1939-40), 221-39. Study of word-play in Heywood; will interest the student of language more than the one of drama. Argues for some connection between Heywood's style and that of Lyly.

YOUNG, KARL. "The Influence of French Farce Upon the Plays of John Heywood: A Criticism of Wilhelm Swoboda," *Modern Philology*, II (1904), 97-124. Important study of Heywood's debt to French farce; answers in detail several of Swoboda's arguments.

ZANDVOORT, R. W. "The Messenger in the Early English Drama," *English Studies*, III (1921), 100-7. Sees Mery-reporte as a messenger—a concrete character derived from court life—not as a vice—an allegorical abstraction.

Index